COASTLINES

COASTLINES

The Poetry of Atlantic Canada

Edited by
Anne Compton
Laurence Hutchman
Ross Leckie
Robin McGrath

GOOSE LANE

Cover illustration: Glaze detail by Peter Powning. Reproduced with permission.
Cover and interior design by Julie Scriver.
Printed in Canada by Transcontinental Printing.
10 9 8 7 6 5 4 3 2

National Library of Canada Cataloguing in Publication

Coastlines : the poetry of Atlantic Canada / edited by Anne Compton . . . [et al.].

Includes bibliographical references and index.
ISBN 0-86492-313-9

1. Canadian poetry (English) — Atlantic Provinces. 2. Canadian poetry
(English) — 20th century. I. Compton, Anne, 1947-

PS8295.5.A85C62 2002   C811'.5408'09715   C2002-903639-9
PR9198.2.A852C62 2002

Published with the financial support of the Canada Council for the Arts,
the Government of Canada through the Book Publishing Industry Development
Program, and the New Brunswick Culture and Sports Secretariat.

Goose Lane Editions
469 King Street
Fredericton, New Brunswick
CANADA E3B 1E5
www.gooselane.com

CONTENTS

COASTLINES

The Poetry of Atlantic Canada

The present renaissance in Atlantic poetry is a cause for celebration. The years since 1995 have seen a remarkable number of highly acclaimed first books from poets such as Tammy Armstrong, Lynn Davies, Sue Goyette, John MacKenzie, Brent MacLaine, Robert Moore, Thomas O'Grady, matt robinson, Sue Sinclair, and Patrick Warner. Second books from writers such as Michael Crummey, Carmelita McGrath, Carole Langille, and Anne Simpson have established the national reputations of these poets. As well, the poets of mid-career have published some of their finest work: Elisabeth Harvor's *The Long Cold Green Evenings of Spring*; Brian Bartlett's *The Afterlife of Trees*; George Elliott Clarke's *Blue*; Don Domanski's *Parish of the Physic Moon*; Douglas Burnet Smith's *The Killed*; Harry Thurston's *If Men Lived on Earth*; Richard Lemm's *four ways of dealing with bullies*; and John Steffler's *That Night We Were Ravenous*. Each of these books is arguably the best work yet from poets whose national significance has been established for some years.

This flowering of Atlantic poetry has been both noticed and rewarded both nationally and internationally. In 2001, George Elliott Clarke won the Governor General's Award for Poetry, and Don Domanski, Lynn Davies, Sue Goyette, and Carole Langille have all been nominated for the award in recent years. Both Brian Bartlett and matt robinson have won the Petra Kenney Poetry Competition. Many Atlantic poets have won national poetry prizes, including the League of Canadian Poets' prizes and various magazine awards. Across Canada people are talking about Atlantic poetry in a way they haven't since the period of Alden Nowlan and Milton Acorn. The oldest literary magazine in Canada, *The Fiddlehead*, established in 1945, heralded the previous Atlantic poetry renaissance of the 1950s and 1960s, the era in which Acorn and Nowlan published the books that made their careers. Poets who were Nowlan and Acorn's contemporaries continue to publish fine books to this day: Tom Dawe, Elizabeth Brewster, Fred Cogswell, Robert Gibbs, Douglas Lochhead, and Michael Thorpe have produced new books since 1995. M. Travis

Lane, whose remarkable career parallels theirs, is the most recent winner of the Atlantic Poetry Prize.

In creating a comprehensive and historical anthology of the past fifty years, the editors offer readers an opportunity to see the lasting effects of that earlier renaissance and to anticipate with us the results of the present one. In doing so, we are mindful of the national force exerted by our still more distant predecessors Charles G.D. Roberts and Bliss Carman, and E.J. Pratt, who in the last decades of the nineteenth century and the first half of the twentieth century propelled a nation into poetry. Our newest generation of Atlantic poets is part of a tradition of Atlantic poetry that has always been an integral thread in the Canadian literary fabric. *Coastlines* articulates the last fifty years of this tradition, balancing the well-established and the just-emerging. Readers will find here the familiar, cherished voices of Alden Nowlan, Milton Acorn, Tom Dawe, Elizabeth Bishop, and John Thompson. And they'll also find fresh new voices.

Since June of 1999, when this project began in the Ice House on the University of New Brunswick campus, the editors have travelled, metaphorically speaking, the coasts and interiors of four provinces. We were astonished by the wealth and variety of the poetry we discovered, and we delighted in how these poets inhabit their particular time and place. We listened to the rhythm of their speech. All of them, in one way or another, "held East under their tongues," to paraphrase Lynn Davies.

The reasons for an Atlantic poetry renaissance are more difficult to identify than the fact of it, but the editors wonder if this flourishing is related in part to a dynamic and changing sense of regionalism. It is perhaps a cliché to talk about the way in which the Atlantic region feels closely tied to a long cultural history of place; nevertheless, its present, these poets tell us, is conversant with its rural past. Although the new regionalism does not abandon the deep connection to the historical and local, it reinterprets the local in the global context and enables a kinetic relationship with cultures and economies around the planet. Proponents of the new regionalism are prepared to rethink the ways in which the Atlantic region can interact with other international regions, ways that allow the local to speak against the global, or to reinterpret the global, when it needs to. All of which enables our area to redefine its relation to other Canadian regions, and in particular to that regionalism that Atlantic Canadians often see as the most parochial, Toronto regionalism.

One sign of the changing dynamic of regionalism is the emergence of Island Studies, an international movement organized for the purpose of studying the unique social and cultural contexts of island communities. In Atlantic Canada it has proceeded from the assumption that Prince Edward Island, Cape Breton, and Newfoundland need to study and learn from the economic and cultural successes of such island nations as Iceland and Ireland, that there might be much to be gained from the greater self-determination in economic and trade policy enjoyed by those countries. More important for *Coastlines*, however, is the further assumption that an island's literature is integral to the articulation of its cultural, social, and economic livelihood.

The redefining of regionalism and the way it is now lived and experienced has caused the editors to think carefully about what constitutes Atlantic poetry. Populations are far more migratory than ever before, and we realized immediately that a definition of the Atlantic poet that required that he or she be born and raised in the region and still be living here would be untenable. There is no definitive calculus for determining what makes a poetry Atlantic, so we made our selections by establishing for a poet one or two of three general criteria: was the poet born and raised here? has the poet spent a good portion of his or her adult life here? and does the poetry reflect the culture or landscape of the region in some significant fashion? After this we did take into account one or two other considerations. The anthology is divided by province and displays the distinctive development of poetry in each of the four provinces. The anthology is also spread across a time from approximately 1950 to the present. We wanted to embrace some of the earliest poetry of our period and so included work from Charles Bruce's last collection, *The Mulgrave Road*, which won the Governor General's Award in 1953. We also wanted to include emergent voices, and so we read the manuscript poetry of Tammy Armstrong, Geoffrey Cook, and Robert Moore. During our deliberations, Armstrong's *Bogman's Music* and Moore's *So Rarely in Our Skins* have been published, and Cook's *Postscript* is forthcoming.

Although the anthology contains many poems about coastlines, the sea, the rural landscape, river valleys, and marshes, and so on, the reader will find poems here that do not have this region as their subject. We were interested first in choosing the best poetry, and we defined *the best* as poetry combining a degree of intellectual and emotional complexity with an exceptional and expressive control of figuration and metaphor, voice and style, syntax, line and line break, rhythm and sound pattern. As editors we realized that if *Coastlines* provides expansive reading pleasure, it is because of the exceptional range of poetic intelligences it represents, because of the ways the poets find of working and reworking the terrain and topography of Atlantic culture and landscape.

One of the secret pleasures of an anthologist is to rediscover and present again the extraordinary talents of poets whose work has been overlooked. *Coastlines* contains the work of the acknowledged luminaries of our region, but there are, in our view, two truly great poets in this anthology who typically go unrecognized. The first is Alfred G. Bailey, one of Canada's foremost modernists, who is at least the equal of F.R. Scott, Dorothy Livesay, or Earle Birney. It is astonishing that his work is slowly disappearing from our national anthologies. Perhaps the publication of this anthology will go some small way toward bringing his work back to national attention. The second is John Smith, a poet as talented as that other modernist metaphysical, A.J.M. Smith, yet John Smith's work seems little known outside of Atlantic Canada. There are other remarkable poets whose work is not sufficiently recognized. Publication of the complete works of Kay Smith would bring this talented poet a wider readership and the attention she deserves. Similarly, new selections of poetry by Robert Gibbs and Peter Sanger would display just how very fine these poets are.

The Atlantic coastline includes many small islands such as Pictou, Grand Manan, and Merasheen, as well as the island provinces of Newfoundland and Prince Edward Island. From the first days of settlement in this country to the present, culture has always moved between the islands and the mainland, and along the coasts or inland from the river mouths. In many ways the Atlantic region *is* an island, a small outcrop far from the centres of power in Quebec, Ontario, and the West, but it is also a place unto itself with a vista onto the farthest reaches of the sea.

NEW BRUNSWICK

Presque Isle, Maine

I want to tell you about the emptiness of Presque Isle:
the potato fields like furrowed foreheads
stretching beyond tin calyxes of garages,
the bus that shrank and finally disappeared
into the hem of the sky.
Standing on Mars Hill, we could look out in ten directions
over nothing but dark soil and the coloured coats
of children running behind ploughshares.
Scooping potatoes from the garden,
they held them to their chests like hedge sparrows.

I want to tell you about the hinged air,
the cold sadness that blew straight through our mitts and scarves —
about the mailman who drove by in an old station wagon,
his mass melting over the front seat
as he extended a gloved hand, pointing
the best side of the hill to go down,
down into the valley with our suitcases and gifts of chocolate,
into the valley where the wind might strum
the power lines into something beautiful.

Boat Builder

Swollen belly of the hull,
ribs nestle between your ill-fitted jeans
while I shuffle through mahogany shavings,
through the planed curls that spell out
the spaces, the rootless pockets of our silence.
The frame moans as you tip it to keel,

speak the body softly,
rub a palm over smoothed sides,
inspect for nicks, for ant galleries.

You've kept me away all these years,
running me to the house to refill three-finger drinks —
a ten-year-old cocktail waitress who wondered
about this hidden world —
half-finished creatures
under crinkled tarpaulins.

Gone now,
an element of summer dusk
dragging the boat over gravel,
sawdust-speckled arm jerking the choke
to urge the outboard purr,
push you through the channel, out beyond
the farthest buoy where gummy moonlight
beads you into a dozen hunched shadows —
a breathing ember, sleepy with rye.

Mother's Winter Guests

The kitchen party voices hesitated
each time a log collapsed in the cast-iron stove —
voices that waited for flames to suffocate beneath damp pine,
for squirming silences to end.
I listened beneath winter coats —
layers of snow-damp wool and fur,
as Mother's gingery banter crept over beer hisses,
over the embarrassed laughter of other sober housewives
who no longer acknowledged drunken flirtations;
their words fell like ice into an always empty tumbler.

Quarters saved for the red dress —
coins in a tea tin filled and hid in the bottom
of the closet, behind photo albums and knitting yarn.
The soft clink all spring — weekly count —
pocket change claimed as her own.
All year, to go without
for a bolt of department store gossamer,
weaving now through stories, unfinished sentences.

Miasma of Drum tobacco, hand creams,
a leaking bottle of cinnamon schnapps in a suit coat,
she peeled me away, led me to my room,
would later beg father to bed,
allowing him to press her small frame,
pull her down while he half-slumped into a rye-thick sleep.
Lie there until dawn then, eyes wide,
face pressed into the sheets of spice
left over from cold winter guests.

Wood Stove Sunday

*The next poem I write will have firewood right
in the middle of it.*
                              — Raymond Carver

Dish-eyed in the basement,
my sister piled walls of pitch pine,
hummed a hymn from the saltbox of a church
we attended every Sunday morning —
three feet between us as we fought
over those frost-heaved hills.
We agreed to hate each other, burn hollows
through supplications, first sermon
before the collection quarters fell

too often from our balanced tongues,
spun over Murphy Oiled floors.
Now we worked in accepted silence,
kept our eyes to the damp earth
while piling winter's wood.

On Wood Stove Sunday we tried to hide along the river,
tried to hide from the inevitable evening:
darning needles, splinters,
our mother steadying our palms in her lap.
But autumn's rust drove us out,
blistered until we could no longer breathe,
until we knew our hands pitchy, raw
to remind us we had come from orchards —
born in the belly of cast-iron stoves,
our vanity was a sin.

Stained from sap and wolf spiders,
we wore rain capes over good sweaters,
whispered library books near the tailgate
while father full of drinking stories
stacked stick after stick into my hooked arms.
Staggering again to the flakeboard chute,
I slid them down slowly
while my sister bowed to each one
before piling the wall higher.

Horse Girls

So you're a horse girl, he says,
smiles as though we are somehow afflicted,
somehow convergent with dark rutted fantasy.
Yes, we are the ones who dream
in pale sparrow grass,

who tick our tongues at the sunfisher,
climb on, barely breathing,
knowing fear could fill a field,
snap a spine like tinder.
We ride bareback
to watch the boys squirm
at the insistence in their minds:
we will always find something to hold on to.

Belly muscles quiver beneath our legs
while the struts of rib cage,
large enough to envelop the sky-licked lake
carry us through backwater country,
out to where we no longer hear the highway,
no longer fear a moment with a gelding,
a hatchback, car horn,
something even the horse girls can't anticipate.

There is memory through tiger lily switchbacks,
a tongue-twist around a bit,
a muzzle soft as deer moss, old denim,
snuffling over a palm, searching
horse girls who smell
of sunburn and barnyard dogs.
No longer child-women,
but extensions of broomtails,
of Sable Island serenity
in love with no one
as we crawl easily over,
urge the gate open with a tanned foot,
gone while the light still holds above.

The Unreturning

Blue is my sky peter
and white my frayed gull.
We had begun to sail
into the milky magma,
the gull's cry
and the moon's tail
beyond the glassy ports and the squeaking cordage
where the long waves leap
and the crests of wind reform their ragged continents.

Voices that cry out at the world's end
or here on the sea's anvil,
fraught with space, will have no ears.
All sights and sounds are a perished wake,
are the lost bearings of the unfound star
which hides no haven in a waxing light.
Attempts to measure the sun's long spoke by day
in a ladder of cloud
will make no way
through the wrinkled shroud.

There will be no world there when we are there,
and no one to know, even the lone hand
at the wheel
whose face is caught in a tanned and wrinkled dream.

Drugged by water and wind
into the dream of the water's vertical eye,
armed with no measure of the fathom's track
we sink and die
and rise again unknown,
and knowing no release
no certain bound,
our misty bodies die and rise

and are nowhere found to us who never cease
and never return to the lost world
or new world found.

The Isosceles Lighthouse

The empty lighthouse stood where the man who built it died.
Skulls, ribs, hips, and thigh-shanks, found there,
      seven in number,
gave it a name to leave alone, and yet —
What was it drew the eye, the questioning thought,
fixed the shape of space between the
      flat-topped dunes and the northwest
capes of gneiss and granite, beetling and seared by fire?
It was the lighthouse, the only object
at the middle point of the gravel island,
isosceles at the middle point of the visible world.
And those who saw it, awake,
felt its presence in sleep
like a concrete unit of mind,
fearful and indispensable, imposing

conditions electric and simple.
They had to go there, those who saw it said,
go to the island, sail through the blurs of mist,
over the racing sea, to arrive without hurt.
But they never got there.
What was thought by them to be the island,
was it the island?
Was it a thing in itself
or a copy of what they had in their minds?
Whatever it was, or whatever it could have been,

it was a focus of force,
        always there,
known and felt by them always.

There at the outward edge of a reef of boulders
dotting the margins of vision
like a faraway herd of huge basking seals
that even the flood tides
                        never were able to cover,

was the island with the lighthouse
standing midway upon it,
the thing, visioned and motionless,
and no sound except the sea,
boiling and racing.

On that isotherm
images of small craft,
canots du nord, sloops, yawls, and dories,
veering and pitching,
swept through their dreams.

La Route Jackman

We went down the long curved hill
"To Canada" it said,
leaving the uninhabited mountains
of the Boundary Range, the ponds
ratched by wind, the General Store
boarded up and left
for the season, or for keeps, it seemed more likely;
    this hard country
Benedict Arnold came over,
in his green sash, on a
day of sleet and rain,
his men haggard and sore, the smallpox
growing in their faces
starved and white with
grit, and lame hands
torn and bleeding from rope burns.

We coasted down the long hill
having climbed high into the mountains
not needing ropes, without need to haul barges
through dead birch thickets and over the scarred tops,
    breaking open hands
like Arnold's men invading Canada
    in seventeen seventy-five, and he
winding up with a musket ball in the knee
at the Sault-au-Matelot barricades.

We coasted, tires whirring
over new pavement, having passed
Penobscot water running back,
ourselves forward towards
the level fields of Beauce,
the populated pasture land,
knowing all at once the feeling
of having come home.

Rivière du Loup

For years and years
for summers and summers without number,
we have looked across the sea at Rivière du Loup.
The lawn in front in too much sun,
but for the sprinkler water,
would have been brown or dun.
The sea water below
with the tide in the sun,
becomes, beyond, a haze of hazy blue.
Beyond was the word that was always sounding
in the sea of the mind.
And those who did not go,
those who did not go,
those who stayed behind,
would rest forever upon the grass
singing the revolving song
Alas! Alas!
If we did not touch them
with the finger of our foremost eye
we'd fail to lift them up to go there too,
with feet in the sea instead of the grass,
with the mind in the sky
set to fly
faithful and willing with us
to that other long look,
that carried us through
that carried us day after day
to Rivière du Loup.

Where I Come From

People are made of places. They carry with them
hints of jungles or mountains, a tropic grace
or the cool eyes of sea gazers. Atmosphere of cities
how different drops from them, like the smell of smog
or the almost-not-smell of tulips in the spring,
nature tidily plotted with a guidebook;
or the smell of work, glue factories maybe,
chromium-plated offices; smell of subways
crowded at rush hours.

Where I come from, people
carry woods in their minds, acres of pine woods;
blueberry patches in the burned-out bush;
wooden farmhouses, old, in need of paint,
with yards where hens and chickens circle about,
clucking aimlessly; battered schoolhouses
behind which violets grow. Spring and winter
are the mind's chief seasons: ice and the breaking of ice.

A door in the mind blows open, and there blows
a frosty wind from fields of snow.

Return of the Native

This is the true land of fairy tales,
this countryside of sullen beauty
heavy beneath dark trees. The brown smell of wood
lingers about it. Sawdust penetrates
every corner. You smell it, mixed with manure,

in the restaurant with its moosehead, or, like dim must,
in the little movie house.

The short street swims in dust and sunshine, slides
into a country road and crosses the bridge
across the log-filled river where men walk,
balancing on the logs, and a single rowboat
holds a group of boys, their dark, round heads
bent close together. Sunshine, wind and water
carry together the floating smell of boards.

Across the bridge is pasture; later, woods.
This is a land
not settled yet by its generations of settlers.
Wildness still lingers, and the unfriendly trees
suffer, but do not shelter, man, their neighbour.
No Eden this, with parks and friendly beasts,
though hopeful settlers, not far distant, called
their country Canaan, New Jerusalem,
or even Beulah. Yet beauty here is solemn,
with the freshness of some strange and morning world.

At the last house on the edge of the woods, two children
sit on their swings, reading aloud to each other
a fairy tale of children in a wood.
Their mother, hanging up her Monday wash,
stops for a minute and watches flying over
the shining crows flapping their heavy wings.

The Moving Image

The natural image is a moving image.

Already the apple blossoms are almost gone,
lilacs (just perceptibly) begin to fade.
The dandelions are their own ghosts

but peonies and roses are budding,
I have planted beets and radishes and lettuce
which I hope may grow later.

The sun's in and out
when the clouds shift.

They shift with the wind.
Birds dart through shrubbery,
scold me, or call for rain.

So small an insect crosses my page
I almost fail to see it.
Would a bird see it?

An ant carries so large a piece of leaf
I think it has wings.
A fat bee lands on a spike of lilac.

Ezra's *Cantos*
make marble seem liquid
something derived from water
or else vegetative, growing
("forest of marble," "pleached arbour of stone").

I read the *Cantos* here in my garden

read a cookbook with a recipe
for "Still-Life Omelette"
which I decide to make for supper.

Valley-Folk

O narrow is the house where we are born,
And narrow are the fields in which we labour,
Fenced in by rails and woods that low hills neighbour
Lest they should spill their crops of hay and corn.
O narrow are the hates with which we thorn
Each other's flesh by gossip of the Grundies,
And narrow are our roads to church on Sundays,
And narrow too the vows of love we've sworn.

But through our fields the Saint John river flows
And mocks the patterned fields that we enclose;
There sometimes pausing in the dusty heat
We stretch cramped backs and lean upon our hoes
To watch a seagull glide with lazy beat
To wider regions where the river goes.

George Burroughs

Although George Burroughs often used a knife,
As farmers must, to castrate or to kill,
He took no pleasure in the touch of steel.
As one who loved to feel things come to life
Beneath his hands, to end the patient strife
Of calving heifers pleased him best of all.
He liked the springtime better than the fall,
But all his farm was fruitful save his wife.

They say that when the doctor came last Spring
And said that he could never have a child,

Although he neither stormed nor acted wild,
He would not let the seed-drill work his lands
But walked the barren fields himself, sowing
The seed broadcast with quick jerks of his hands.

The Water and the Rock

Hard rock was I, and she was water flowing,
Over sharp stones of opposition going;
Shaping herself to me as to a cup,

She filled the valleys of my ego up
With a cool, smooth compliance, everywhere
As yielding and unhurtable as air.

Soft was my love as water, and I forgot
In the calm wash of compliant rhythm caught
How water shapes and softens, sculpts and smoothes
The channel of the rock through which it moves.

The Beach at Noon

Full-faced to the brisk sea gale, I breathe air
Cold, sharp, and salt as the white-edged waves
And see the same sea-silver on gulls' wings
That slip the driving wind. Above me now
The sun's noon glory hangs, reminding me
There is some brightness that no eyes can bear.

On the bay's other side the cliffs are bare,
Then sudden flower in the lambent air
Rose-red against the double blue of waves
And sky. But even as I watch them now
Their glow already seems less bright to me
Who in this moment feel my lack of wings.

Fixed on this spot even as the wind wings
Up cloud and shape-dissolving rain, I bear
The pain of seeing now a scene I know
I am a part of patterned in the air
With all of air's fragility — cliff, waves,
Sun, sky, gull wings one instant fused in me!

Although the core of consciousness is me,
The power is otherwhere. Outside are wings
Of wind and gull, are sun, cliff, sky, and waves
That, despite my hope and memory, bear
Their kaleidoscopic patterns in the air,
Intent upon an ever-moving *now*.

I command a world within, active now
As words and symbols weave their spells for me,
But it's tied too tight to the outer air
By sense impressions, and the flying wings
Of every thought are clipped by the bare
Hard knife of fact that around them waves.

It is when my current and the world's waves
Blend in one billow, as they did just now,
That their imbalance is so hard to bear.
There is this difference between things and me:
Things know no pattern; like chaff winnowings
They drift wherever force directs the air.

On wings of wind, the rain squall drives the waves.
The air above grows dark. Outside me now
The discord lays my limitations bare.

After Rain

We walk to the garden where the old rhubarb flourishes. New leaves on trees; my mother's long dress lifts in wind. She bends over rhubarb, the tall, thick stems, the leaves like umbrellas. She says she has never seen it so rich, so green — as if someone gardened here.

My father dead three months now. He turns a clod of earth, watches an earthworm disappear . . . For him there is no house here, no car, only green meadows going on and on . . . and there are no people: only when my mother rises to walk between the trees does he feel a presence like the stillness after rain.

The Worker Bee

My mother hands me the still form of a worker bee. It is strangely silent in my palm, curled in on itself, as if asleep. I'm careful with it at first, for I remember the sudden heat of the stinger. But this yellow and black bee, striped near the rump, once as feared as a lion, won't sting again. I feel a sadness holding it, for it is like anything that has lived and died — what you miss most is the motion, the supple flow of moving form. I look at the face: it is shaped a bit like a sheep's, coal black, only shinier, reflective as polished stone. And the wings are stained glass in a monk's room, or a map on the wall, sketching the steep paths of the air.

I pick her up by one wing and shake her. She rattles like ripe seeds inside a pod. The whir of wings is reduced to this single sort of sound, abrupt and sharp, like castanets shaken by someone mourning a death. Perhaps this is the sound of the honey stomach, now dry like all the other organs, but still holding a sweetness that never got back to the hive.

And maybe inside there is amber, and if I opened her now
the scent of honey would rise from the body casket, and
the many eyes on the face would remember flowers, bright
spring flowers, clover and dandelion, their colours in June —
and other colours known only to the bee, ultraviolet, yellow
and blue.

In the Beginning

In the beginning was the highway. Knitting needles and variegated
brown-yellow wool in my pack, distance on folded paper.

Twice you found me waiting by the road. I dreamed sock but knit a hole
in the tire. So many wildflowers I couldn't name. Our silence.

Like a leaf, the canoe. Unravelled early fall up a lake. Dusk-
foolish moose and her calf, the white lights fluid above us.

Innocent, we cast off into waves pouring walls on the beach.
Wind culled paddling, hummocky moss dead end. The map forgot us.

By the orange spotted touch-me-not. Or jewelweed. We drove south
through the badlands. When I cut the yarn, my sock fit a giant.

Cape Enrage

Only a picture from a blue tin box.
                              The day
we shared lunch on a blanket over stones, my mother
pouring from a thermos, steam curling like smoke,
the cocoa dark as the Fundy tide relinquishing the flats,
        exposed mud shiny as a giant's mirror.
My footprints trekking through clouds and sky,
searching for the spot where the tide turns.

                              In the picture
I wear the moss-green jacket my mother sewed for me.

Hold my father's hand under a cliff, in the cave
he told me never dried out between tides.
Then the slow drive down a dirt road so narrow
        we had to shut windows to keep out the leaves,
        frantic as trapped insects against the glass.
Onto the lined, somnolent pavement
leading inland to bed where I lay thinking
of that cave full of ocean,
all entrance gone.

When Ships Sail Too Close

When a storm turns the corner, she wonders where to look,
at the raindrops on the window, or the wreckage outside.
Snow resigned to slush, the rain pulling rivers
from driveways, braiding currents down the roads.
The farther she looks, the more she thinks she

might know and understand. How icebergs grow,
and the evolving thoughts of people in cars
stalled in the lakes fed by the rivers. She's heard
that the eyes of old sea captains stay strong,
searching the horizon for lost ships, weather, and land.
One summer she saw the dusky ocean

meet way out there a line of metallic gold so hot
it would ignite any ship that sailed too close.
Now branches take root in the wind,
strain the silent arms holding the ground together.
In the rain-speckled window beside her,
reflections — a lamp, a pillow, two children playing.

When You Can't Leave Me Anymore

The day you fly to Tennessee, the snow
begins to fall. April snow berating the crocuses
and tulips, falling as if it cannot stand
for another minute the ground warming up
in early spring. At dusk, our children go out to play.
They build a snowman, work together in a wind
that rearranges our backyard. He props up the head
while she punches in a carrot nose.
Pulls off his mittens to press popsicle sticks
into a v-shaped grin. She finds pebble eyes
and tree-branch arms spread wide.
    I watch them play so I can tell you
when you come home how the bodies we made
are still close in their short time together.
I think of death, when spring storms will rage on
without me, when you can't leave me anymore.
My memories of you and them broken
like those flakes filling the air.
Pieces of me and what I remember
carried off in my children and you
going places I won't know.

On the Train

For Helen, the journey is not complete without bridges
and their possibilities. Imagine the train falling
when the trestle breaks over the Shepody River
like it did three years before she was born.
The crew and seven passengers living to tell the tale,
including a woman who claims she was guided from the coach
by her lately departed husband's ghost calling to her

from the salt grasses. Now Helen watches trees deep as water
flow by her window, a picture on a page she never has to turn.
This train carries her and her mother and brother
to where the brown river muscles the mud banks
far apart, the river sensing something bigger
than itself. They are met by family at Hillsborough
for a short vacation, the air cooler here.
Helen watches the train pull away
towards the bridge she knows they never rebuilt.
Tore up the tracks, leaving coastal villages like Alma,
with its low-tide glistening beach, alone
on a trail they called a road. Like her mother,
so quiet since they carried the dead boy home,
stalled on a private road neither can name
or find on a map.

All this night long

All this night long and longer
I've been taking inventory of
country roads   and sometimes less
than roads   tracks and logging ruts and
blazes all but healed over
all the ways of getting from the centre
of this woods to that point
along the shore   that place where
a light beams out and a horn
thickens through inblowing fog

All of them over rough tracts past
raw slashes and green newgreen in
burnt over humus and blueberry patches

Sometimes after a single man
on foot   along rivers and off them
up steep brooks   seeing him step
round or jump over logs and stumps
into staghorn moss or wild mushrooms

Seeing him break his way or wade
long enough to know the motions
he makes with his head and hands
cocking ears at a bird call or
stooping over a pebble bed for one
to turn in his hand   or toss
two or three times before giving
it back with a giving all his own

In and out of counties   across
borders   through swamps and flooded out
intervals   slogging all night long to
make connections more connected   to say

See how it all radiates   or how
it all assembles   to say
Hey you there   insisting you are
there   Hey I have you here

And that gentle plodder   parting
many thicknesses is no more apart
from you than you from me

A Kind of Wakefulness

You've left no door or I'd knock
you sacked in your silk house
bug worm   whatever you are
so there's no getting in or I'd come
and wrap myself in your fine suspense
breathing as the earth breathes
once or twice a winter

Maybe it's a way of getting wings
to spread in a big spring show

slowing down that much
taking winter for what it is

these days when the westerlies
shake teeth loose
and needle eyelids through
as if to stitch them up

Or I'd join a bear in dreams
exchanging my spirit maybe
with some astral anti-bear
who'd amble the night sky wide awake

while my head joined numb ground
under a heaved up stump
in a fellow heaviness

dreaming likely
of green caves under the sun
where in August heat raspberry canes
bent together
light their cool spaces
with heavy sweet combed fruit

Dreaming what the earth dreams
breathing to its bass
must be a kind of wakefulness
sharper-eyed
than this fleeced and muffleheaded
snow blindness

The Death of My Father

My father died Christmas Eve in
the middle of the night and
the green breath of the big tree
in our frontroom mixed with
the dark smell of death upstairs.
My mother called us in and said
"I think he's gone, your father's gone," and
seeing the slack black gape
of his mouth, I thought of the cold
bluebodied turkey in the fridge downstairs.

A praiseworthy man, on Sundays out to meeting
with praise of God in his eyes and not
a pigeon missed with breadcrumbs nor

a dicky-bird in the gutter   and not
a tomcat passed with his ruff
unruffled or his rough purr unpurred.
A man simple enough, in love with sunsets
and butter-and-eggs by the railway tracks
where we took our Sunday walks around
the waterfront and afterwards reformed
baptist hymns which his thick fingers pressed
from the thick strings of his cello.

I see you dad, on your high stool in
your shop, eyeglass wrenched into play and
fine curly gold turning up and off from
your keen graver as you cut "Love for
always and always" on the inside circus
of a secondhand wedding ring.
And how we hoarded the dust from
every sweeping in a tall black can and
shipped it away to the refiner to have
your gold and silver letters, all
your days' cuttings from coffin plates
and babyspoons, cradled out
in his white secret fire and
sent back, sent back.

This Catching of Breath at the Top

I hear a clock strike   a hammer
hammering   and a robin's urgings
I hear my own breath in this breathless

standstill   this midsummer dark   .
lit from inside every
dripping leaf   The pine outside

my window's wick'd with new
ten-to-twelve inch wicks
Ten marigold lamps light the

sprout-beds   set there to
set back the resident groundhog
Fog and drizzle pace all

breathing to a vegetable speed
Standoffs   arrests stalemates   infest
inaudible and invisible currents and cross

currents   those unstoppable warbles no
warbler at his or her business
pays attention to   After

today I know which way my
garden will turn   I know how soon
in all this green liquefaction

I'll taste oxalic needles
This catching of breath at the top
is like that catching of breath

at the bottom   a turn in the dance
I live in   and live by   one that
will go on turning after every

clock in the house has struck and
every carpenter has hammered every
nail   fast   home

The Manes P. Aground Off Fort Dufferin

The wariness of the ship resting there
is like a bird's leaning off one wing
favouring what's broken

She waits while the tide waits
and the slack washes out
secrets of a temper

that tore out her anchor
with high white shatterings of itself
and banged her steel hull

against the breakwater all one night
reiterating the dark
doubly dark

The way she sits high
on her shoulder's angle
decks lighting up as the sun drops red

you'd think she'd right herself
on her second wind
and move off easy

But she'll stay   her uneasiness
a thing
to move in the mind

till the next storm takes up her pounding
and the next after the next
breaks her up.

ELISABETH HARVOR

Four O'Clock, New Year's Morning, New River Beach

You hear him cry in the
dark. The air smells of floor wax,
cold duck fat, the tree
shedding its needles down into the
room whose bay window looks out
on the winter ocean. You even think you can hear,
above the roof's peak, how the new
snow is steadily falling
on the ice crust of the old year.

You feel for your kimono,
to the right of a hulk of sleeping
shoulder, the dark hull of a husband
going down in a sleep-floe. You
cross the floor to the cold window;
see a snowfall of soot falling
between your mother-in-law's house
and the boathouse, the only white flakes
flying into the cone of light

shining down on the ice-glazed path to the beach.
Shivering, you yawn down at the snowed-on lawn
as you wrap one half of your kimono over the
other half, like a thought of something sombre
you long ago promised yourself you'd remember.

Out of the Bay of Fundy night
it comes back to you: the vow to be less bitter, happier,
a different person. You pad through
the white cottagey gloom of the cold hallway;

old summer clothes spy on you — a once-brave
bathing suit, now salt-faded and puckered,
a scarecrow-short raincoat, smelling of rubber

and the beach. Now you're close enough to hear
him start to coo in response to your sleepy
progress of creaks. He is small
and audacious, and so you imagine
you can imagine what he is imagining: that
the two of you are in league, cahoots,

two lovers in love with the night.
In answer, your breasts start to
prick with new milk, making small
moons of damp on the kimono's pale silk. When you
duck into his low loft, he waves his legs,
he's so happy to see you. You lift him up,
hitch him onto a hip, take him to the window
to see the way the soot-snow
is falling in front of the

snow-snow
steadily, steadily.
He's so sleep-flushed! His hair is
damp grass still warm from his pillow,
his leggings have been
knit out of curdled white string,
his nightgown's a dwarf's surplice — roses
washed till they look like clover,
made littler, reduced
by time and detergent
are falling
through
the new year's fogged
sleeping dimness.

The Damp Hips of the Women

Two weeks before
the end of the war
with Japan, I climbed
with my mother and four
of her friends up the path
from the beach, up the long
aisle of shivering poplars,
I remember spandex
and paisley

expanding, contracting
on the damp hips of the women,
but it would have had to be some other
fabric back in those edgy days of

pale sunshine and fog — not spandex
but some sort of elasticized jersey,
the air smelling of decay, effervescence,
damp birth or death of the earth,

one of the women walking
with the arms of her orange cardigan
tied into a broken-necked knot
on one hip, making her oiled back
end in an uneven and cocky orange apron
    worn backwards
its jaunty sway back and forth

and me with a river
of sand embedded in the
flowered crotch of my swimsuit
    along with a deeper
worm of wrong down in the divided
pudge between my babyish thighs;
    my body

feeling shivery, peppy, as if it
could make me want to cry out "I love you!"

(or "I hate you!")
or suppose I had startled the world
by yelling out "Hip!" Would the women
have waited then, for two more hips to follow?
And for the two hips that followed
to be followed by a shy and frail hooray?

Or I might have shamed myself
utterly by crying out *breast!*

At nine, I couldn't imagine
ever being anything but a lover
of women, I loved the way
they smelled of the hurtful
suction of their wet bathing caps,
their earrings

pressed tight
to their ears by their
white rubber bonnets,

loved the way they
kept swinging backwards

into the river,
sinking slowly back
into deeper water

to laugh
like women in love

at the dipped
coldness,

loved their yelps
of belonging laughter,

loved the slits of winter-white
skin that flashed from the tops
of their brown thighs as they sat
and smoked out on the end of the dock

and then bent over to cry out,
helplessly caught in the adult pain
of amusement, loved their nailpolish
and the sun-paled tan

weave of their borrowed
sandals and their bracelets'
jingles, loved their lives.

　　　*　　*　　*

Somewhere, beyond sky
or river, they are all

still in their damp swimsuits
and still all laughing and climbing
up into the grove of excitable
poplars, mounting the path
in sprung single file.

But no, it's before
even that,

the long afternoon
graduating itself into twilight

while the five
are still holding out
at the far end of the dock
for a final low gossip,

that last peaceful malice,
wigwammed by towels, a last cigarette.

Poem Upon the Forcible Entry by Cat into a Poem Originally Upon Trilliums

A white cat splendid in trilliums
    is a thorough pest,
though lovely, abstract, as the ink brush flow on white paper
    of a modern Zen
painting; undoubtedly equally white and black
    and handsome, when making a nest
of poems, or teething on my black Japanese
    ballpoint pen.
Not everyone chews over my poems for hours
    with such thorough, savouring zest;
the verse will survive, I'd like to think,
    but how to defend the flowers
from criticism so stoutly held, so ardently addressed?
    This scholarly mind, fatigued with rest,
determined, at least, that I shouldn't loaf, he
    scours both yard and page advising:
    ·   iamb, anapest, catastrophe.

Codicil
Including the cost of a monument and inscription

No monument. Let me be ash
thrown out to tide
among the rags and flotsam of the shore
and the severed beads of the bladderwrack.
Or drop from a dory a brown glass jar
weighted with sand for the barnacles

to reach their gritty fingers toward
and tumble in the oil-ooze of the flats.

The inscription: that foamy trace
when tide turns and the osprey from her perch
turns also, or,
where a salmon leaps, or where
the sleek unsaying hides a loon.
No epitaph. Even a stone
returns to the nest of processes.

As for the soul,
nothing will hold or mark it but the same
impermanent elation, heart to heart, a word,
like a live fish in water, sometimes shows.

For Brigid

Out past the airfield there's a house,
close to the road, which for two years
seemed empty: doors locked, windows boarded,
grass erasing the gravel drive.

The third year
the yard sprang up in tamarack,
shaggy, lime green. One room upstairs
peeked through its sagging shutter.
The back door
swung open. An inside wall
was completely repatterned with messages.

The front door fell the following year.
It was open house thereafter: voles, bats,
marmots in the shed, mice nesting in

the old car-seated sofa where
vandals and lovers took their turns.

The windows were shot out, one by one.
Even the roof withdrew its shade,
season by season, til overhead
the bird stars of the summer shone
among the rafters like white moths; the moon
hung from the chimney, familiar.

At home to everything, this house has changed.
It has erased
all that we wanted to think of it
for things that do not remember us.

It is as if a book were closed.
We have lost our place.

Portobello

Walking the railroad-right-of-way
by Portbello Creek: in spring
among the squirrel-tail willows
thick with birds; in summer,
by beaded buckwheat vines,
wild rose, wild flag, anemones,
cow lilies like dogs' lost tennis balls,
and water meadows, rarely hayed —

Each spring the rain sorts out the sand:
links, hooks, spikes, lawn chairs,
general debris. The froggy ditches
fill with trash — a dead horse, once, its hooves
fox-gnawed, its head in a roll of carpeting.

Past the red quarry a hunter's path
leads down from the trackway to the bush —
a cabin barely visible. Was it his horse?
I saw it once among the trees, white,
awkward, untethered, a shade in shades.

Floods have taken the bridge away.
Below the piers black water flows
with an unhurried violence.
On the other side
the white sand ridge of the right-of-way
moves crescent into the darknesses.

This fall we come again to watch
our shadows tremble in the creek
among the floating, tarnished leaves.
The meadows have bleached, dissolving in mists.
Winter to come: the snow, the ice
stacked up against the reeds
with slanting, cracked, and rattling panes,
and, at our usual halting place,
the water, running.

Next winter, will we come so far? The brittle trees,
spruce with their browning needles, stars
glimpsed through the metal-speckled nights,
the snow, the rabbits' dash to ground,
the browning soot of cattails — all
seem much or more or less the same
each year, though our
reflections on that mirror flow
grow feebler, fade.

Sometimes,
I see you as you used to be: thigh deep in brush,
retracing the old buggy paths, lost trails
for moccasin or fox — you read them
on the clambered earth, crisscross
beneath the loggers' ruts, or the hive-mound

logs left out to rot. Now
even this razed and gravelled way
seems long, its end unreachable.
Will we walk to that broken bridge again,
or, dreaming, find it whole?

The Cemetery at Loch End, Catalone, Cape Breton

Long grass of summer held back by wire fence
but on the inside it was all fresh cut
and we did not think, then, of what stroke
or, whatever, cut the sleepers down who lay
beneath, but we were respectful, careful,

walking along the rows of leaning headstones
in our kangaroo jackets and sneakers damp
with sea-dew where the lawn's path led us on
to read inscriptions, to say the names and ages
out loud, repeating almost chanting on the morning wind.

There was only the cut-back forest and passing
tourists bound for Louisbourg and out beyond
fog and sea, hidden as the sleepers were. It
was that way as we knelt and touched with fingers
the lichen-bitten lines of those graven images.

And for one Sarah Jane: "What I say unto you,
I say unto all, watch." We as watchers
made note of the marble and the message,
and one John Nicholson said: "Take ye heed, watch and
pray for ye know not when the time is."

When we prepared to leave we were quiet
there at Loch End. We had been told to wait,
to watch, to pray, but not to weep for them,
for those Presbyterians in Catalone,
Sarah Jane and Katie, Alex, Neil and John.

Nothing

Now, this beginning
at my stage
is agony knowing
only
that out of nothing
the bruise of knowing
only that there is so much
to lay down, put aside
in all of this bush
of life gone whichway
is the agony.

I want only a room
small, white walled
the cross comes
with each sun
through the eastern window.

On bare boards do I kneel
with my insides a storm
of past but now
I must begin
clearing all away
to begin is now
from nothing.

John Thompson

at old St. Ann's at Westcock, the church,
the green cloth with the cross outlined in gold
covers the coffin pine plain as written down,

and inside, as written down, John
in his red-black hunting jacket, his climbing boots,
the 19th century Bible he was given
by the Departmental Secretary heavy it is
with rich lithographs, and the single broadside
with the 100th Psalm *Jubilate Deo*
and he went to find his black panther
the one he said was seen at Jolicure
black hairs caught on the wire fencing
There's a panther out there "pointing," right
out there a black panther, a big black one,
and John will be buried in the pine box
at Jolicure when the cemetery there
is ready next month or so.

John with his silver cross and the bear's tooth
on his neck chain, that was the way
he said he wanted it, knowing where death was.

from The Golden Book of Bovinities

We are nowhere near as calm as we probably appear.
It's just that our minds are elsewhere.

Pound for pound, our eyes are no more expressive
than puddles of dark brown glass.

From the highway they imagine us
nosing toy cars through the grass.

There's just no getting around the fact that certain mornings
in the dew-wet fields are better than others.

When they lean over the fence to shout "moo" at us
it isn't nonsense we shout back.

Breeds are named for places, which is why the Holstein
keeps coming up with maps of anywhere else.

Only when skin develops a sense of industry
will it truly fit like a glove.

On the way to slaughter we advise keeping your head down
and your thoughts pretty much to yourself.

The heart of even an undersized cow
still makes quite a handful.

As evening approaches, discussion inevitably turns
to the topic of greener pastures.

Among other things, Prince Edward Island is famous for its cows.
The bitterness of its horses alone must be spectacular.

Keep your money in your horns. It's the last place
they think to look.

On more than one occasion men have used us for sexual intercourse.
We must seem the very souls of discretion. At least from behind.

Pigs have a saying: *There are no ironists in the abattoir*.
For pigs, that's not bad.

It is widely believed that even our tongues end up on their plates.
Naturally, our feelings on this subject are very difficult
to put into words.

Room with a view

Late into every night, Penelope carefully undid almost that whole
   day's work,
then slept with her fingers moving deep within herself to keep them
   supple;
that was the best and most dangerous secret of all.

The design of the tapestry never varied but each day she was a little
   different;
thus by degrees she flourished and the suitors had only their suspicions;
that was the secret every woman knew.

All those years, she stood for absent husbands, keeping other men
   at a distance,
and the endless opportunities open to an intelligent woman left on
   her own
in a small apartment above reproach.

When Penelope looked at Telemachus, she saw only his father's
   faraway eyes;

when Telemachus looked at Penelope he was sure he saw right
   through her.

The subject of the tapestry was tapestry. Only her women understood,
but even they thought it pornographic because it so excited them.

Odysseus filling the doorway, brilliant in the blood of every available
   rival,
took one look at it and said, *I see. I'll wait for you downstairs.*
Well that's it, she said to herself. *I'm finished. And what would be the
   point*
after all, now that he's home? But then she just sat there, staring at
   her work,
hands at a loss,
                        eyes swimming through seas of their own.

The Skin You Wore

The skin you wore through cortisone years
has thinned to almost nothing now,
a papery set of veils that barely holds
the muddled, berried flesh of legs and arms.

We never thought we'd see you down
to so few and such awful careful steps.
But you will forget the harm in moving
as you used to through the world, until

flowers open on your clothes.
So when you go, I promise I will not say
"She died," but that I knew a woman
of skin so fine she stepped out of it

one day before we even realized.

And He Wept Aloud, So That the Egyptians Heard It

In my grandfather's house
for the first time in years,
houseflies big as bumblebees
playing crazy football
in the skim-milk-coloured windows,

leapfrogging from
the cracked butter saucer
to our tin plates of
rainbow trout and potatoes, catching the bread
on its way to our mouths,
        mounting one another
        on the rough deal table.

It was not so much their filth
as their numbers and persistence and —
oh, admit this, man, there's no point in poetry
if you withhold the truth
once you've come by it —
        their symbolism:
        Baal-Zebub,
god of the poor and outcast,

that enraged me, made me snatch the old man's
Family Herald, attack them like a maniac,
lay to left and right until the window sills
overflowed with their smashed corpses,
until bits of their wings
stuck to my fingers,
until the room buzzed with their terror . . .

And my grandfather, bewildered and afraid,
came to help me:
        "never seen a year

when the flies were so thick"
as though he'd seen them at all before I came!

His voice so old and baffled and pitiful
that I threw my club into the woodbox and sat down
  and wanted to beg his forgiveness
as we ate on in silence broken only
by the almost inaudible humming
of the flies rebuilding their world.

The Red Wool Shirt

I was hanging out my wash,
says the woman in North Sydney.
It was a rope line I was using
and they were wooden pins,
the real old-fashioned kind
that didn't have a spring.

It was good drying weather.

I could see the weir fishermen
at work.
  I had a red wool shirt
in my hands and had just
noticed that one of the buttons
was missing.

Then I looked up and saw
Charlie Sullivan coming
towards me.
He'd always had a funny walk.
It was as if he was walking
sideways.

That walk of his
always made me smile except
for some reason
I didn't smile
that day.
        He had on a hat
with salmon flies
that he'd tied himself
in the brim.

Poor old Charlie.

It's bad, Mary, he said.

I finished
hanging up the red wool
shirt
        and then I said,
Charlie, it's not
both of them, and he said,
Mary, I'm afraid it is.

And that was that.

Britain Street
   Saint John, New Brunswick

This is a street at war.
The smallest children
battle with clubs
till the blood comes,
shout "fuck you!"
like a rallying cry —

while mothers shriek
from doorsteps and windows
as though the very names
of their young were curses:

"Brian! Marlene!
Damn you! God damn you!"

or waddle into the street
to beat their own with switches:
"I'll teach you, Brian!
I'll teach you, God damn you!"

On this street,
even the dogs
would rather fight
than eat.

I have lived here nine months
and in all that time
have never once heard
a gentle word spoken.

I like to tell myself
that is only because
gentle words are whispered
and harsh words shouted.

Daughter of Zion

Seeing the bloodless lips, the ugly knot of salt-coloured hair,
the shapeless housedress with its grotesque flowers
like those printed on the wallpaper in cheap rooming houses,
sadder than if she wore black,

observing how she tries to avoid the sun,
crossing the street with eyes cast down
as though such fierce light were an indecent spectacle:
if darkness could be bought like yard goods
she would stuff her shopping bag with shadows,

noting all this and more,
who would look at her twice?
What stranger would suspect that only last night
in a tent by the river,
in the aisles between the rows
of rough planks laid on kitchen chairs,
before an altar of orange crates,
in the light of a kerosene lantern,
God Himself, the Old One, seized her in his arms and lifted her up
    and danced with her,
and Christ, with the sawdust clinging to his garments and
    the sweat of the carpenter's shop
on his body and the smell of wine and garlic on his breath,
drew her to his breast and kissed her,

and the Holy Ghost
went into her body and spoke through her mouth
the language they speak in heaven!

Day's End
(for Anne)

I have worked since daylight in the hayfields.
We walked home at dusk, following the horses.
For supper, I ate hot bread and spiced ham,
        onions and tomatoes.
Now I kneel over a basin of cold water
and a woman washes my hair —

a strong woman whose knuckles rake my scalp.
Her hands smell of soap, I am naked to the waist,
     she leans her weight against me;
laughs huskily when I seize her wrists
     and try to push away her hands.
I am young and strong but a great weariness is upon me —
I would be willing to die now if I were sure that death is sleep.

Saturday Afternoon

The somnolence of shoes
in shop windows; even the light
doesn't reach them, bounces off
and is escorted away before it can cause
embarrassment. There's no need
for a scene, a calm and plain refusal
is essential. Cool
and composed, they maintain themselves
in a dimly-lit interior, only half
thinking, giving merely the impression
of thought. Don't, they say, don't,
like all things behind glass. They look
over your head, purposeful, averted
gazes, as though seeing a brilliant
and hazy future you can't achieve
but might, if only they looked at you
that way. But you are fallible, you have loved
too much. There is nothing to be done
about this; you are too much like the light.

Red Pepper

Forming in globular
convolutions, as though growth
were a disease, a patient
evolution toward even greater
deformity. It emerges
from under the leaves thick
and warped as melted plastic,

its whole body apologetic:
the sun is hot.

Put your hand on it. The size
of your heart. Which may look
like this, abashed perhaps,
growing in ways you never
predicted.

It is almost painful
to touch, but you can't help
yourself. It's so familiar.
The dents. The twisted symmetry.
You can see how hard it has tried.

Orpheus Meets Eurydice in the Underworld

Still limping, she has come. She waits at the foot of the hill, doesn't
dare go any further, remembers how it once vanished under her
feet.

She has spent the time thinking about her wedding day, tracing the
mark on her ankle where the serpent bit. It hasn't healed yet;
perhaps it won't until he comes back. She has never desired his
death, but wished for it as one wishes for rain.

The steep hill, where it led and couldn't lead. So many times.

When he arrives he looks more tired than she can understand. The
lyre has vanished; they stand together silently.

Even as she remembers his face, she loses something else. She has
been alone so long now; how often she has stood here, how much
she has wanted to climb.

She takes him home, puts him to bed, then slips in beside him. His childhood bed, too short for him now; they will have to find another.

They waken slowly. As ghosts they pass through each other's bodies, she puts her hand into his heart. He had been worried she would forget.

They play in the fields, run races, drift through tall grasses carelessly, as only those who have had to wait forever can. They have a private sign language; no one speaks in this place, even the streams are silent.

Sometimes when they are walking she teases him, falls behind. He looks over his shoulder again and again: there she is. They never tire of this game.

The Refrigerator

Its life is longer
than you ever guessed;
it has travelled further
from what it knows. At night
it looks through the window
to its distant
relatives, the stars. They hum
to one another. Discuss
concepts of time
we don't understand.

When you come home
in the afternoon, it listens
to your troubles, the celibate
friend to whom you confide

everything, steadfast, the eternal
roommate whose sexless,
guileless life is comfort.

You never know how it longs
for intelligent conversation,
can't wait for you
to sleep so it can think
of something besides the lemon
hardening at the bottom
of the crisper. But it has learned
patience.

With a certain grace, a swimmer
waiting for the plunge. Solid,
rectangular, it faces the world
without regrets. It keeps
to itself, won't sleep
on the end of your bed,
but it watches. Reliable,
dependable. The habits
of an introvert: it knows when
to turn itself on and off.

Paddling

The shine, the square of light on every leaf,
lilies, more leaves, the V of the canoe
in the water: gateway
to nowhere, the beginning of imagining you aren't.

Fear of profusion: where things are few, they seem
necessary. The world a hospice, the trees and their thousand leaves
on the verge of disappearance.

Light clamps onto us, we'll have to skin ourselves
to be rid of it. Paddles dip in the water, dip and pretend
they don't know what goes on. Innocence is easiest, but easy to
overdo.

In the mind's mud, nothingness spawns. Where time becomes less
pressing, we feel its depth. The world is burnished, trees, bark, skin
going up in flame. The gods are not what you hoped them to be.

The sun, taking us all down with it.
The ten thousand things, superfluous.

Lilacs

For those who have lived
where lilacs bloom, who have lost
their immunity
                    to idleness and wander through
doorway after doorway
when the lilac trees open their infinite
mauve rooms. For those
who give in and glide a little behind
their lives, a hand trailing
in the water
behind a rowboat.

Regret turns itself inside
out, like a glove
you've picked up after someone's
gone. Even the bees feel it,
sadly, sadly,
nose in the flowers,

a curtain pulled away
and there's no hand on your shoulder
to catch you before you lean too far
out the window.

A slow leak, something escaping
as soon as the petals open.
What's left grows twice
as heavy, pales,
sinks inside itself and stays
with you, a dream of which
there is not even enough left
to describe:

It is about to rain.
It is always about to rain.
These limp flowers.

On Sundays in Summer

On Sundays in summer when I was a child,
  The air was gold all over in one unfolded wing.
  I waded deep in grass and heard the church bells ring,
  And wildflowers spilt their small enamelled gaze on everything.

Ladies' heels clicked softly in the hushed, prim street.
Prayer books blinked, gilt-edged, on white kid gloves.
I thought there was nothing more like little folded doves
Peeping out of sun-splotched taffeta sleeves.

The streetcars had Sunday manners. They made a faint sound
Like dim waves breaking on a Bible-picture shore;
Bliss was sucking peppermints, as ladies stirred the air
Into lovely coloured breezes when the world was young in war.

Again with Music

Now that the rain is spent,
Trees and the purple-headed timothy and the tall grasses
Are all netted over with seed pearls.
Far as the eye can reach the sea is pale as a pearl,
The air a pool of stillness,
And so still the wild roses their petals make porcelain faces.

From leaf to leaf a raindrop slips,
Stillness upon stillness.

And sprawling over the living grass and the roses,
A dead apple tree with beauty in its bare bones,

Never to put forth again a pink and white cloud of witnesses,
Suddenly blossoms with yellow birds in its grey limbs,
And is almost alive again with music.

Love, O Love, let the birds happen to me.
Let the wild, sweet voices remember me.

Remembering Miller
(*for Miller Brittain*)

Touching my face
with your artist's fingers,
you said one day when we were young:
Never be afraid of growing old,
you have such good bones.

Now I am old
but the bones do not comfort me.
Yours matter to you even less
for hollow as they are,
where you lie, the wind has no chance
to make music with them or conversation.

Dear friend, you do not need the bones,
music or conversation with the wind,
nor does the world.

Your new body is the work,
it is your presence among us,
celebrant upon canvas.
This life of yours
glows before our eyes
as once, in all its colours, cadences,
it leapt and danced

raged and wept,
and more than this
reached out beyond itself
and will do so
long after all of us lie where your body lies.

It was in the reaching beyond
I knew you best,
I know you in my bones.

Old Women and Love

Drowning
no end to it

Yeats should have discovered Byzantium
as no country for old women
yet they refuse to die
they clutter up the earth
the blood of old women continues to cry out
to sing even to dance wildly in their veins
Sometimes the blood of an old woman rustles
like a startled bird when love's stealthy step
cracks the dry undergrowth in the frosty air
as if a firecracker were exploding

It seems that love is a hunter of undiscriminating taste
Women old enough to know better — though God is never old
    enough —
dream deeper and deeper into the wood
like the misty-eyed girls they once were
Suddenly one will stop astounded as the trap
love has set closes its steel jaws on a foot of frail bones

This morning very early in this silent house of sleepers
when my eyes opened from the mercy of my own darkness
the world came at me like a blow
Its beauty burned gold in every resurrected leaf
burned with a still flame   Spring never relents
What was I doing here?   What *was* I doing here?
Behind the house the trees slept paired in their cool shadows

At night an old woman on her narrow bed
probing the dark with a stubborn mind
demanding answers she knows she will not find
tends with a fierce joy the unextinguished embers
of a not so temperate love

Horse

Your great hooves sunk
　　in red mud, massive,
　　　　still, you stare out

over the edge of the world;
　　small fires
　　　　flare in your eyes;

the sun turns in hunger
　　about your dark head,
　　　　sniffing the earth in you,
tasting your smoke,

and waits for your thighs
　　to shift, your hooves
　　　　to strain from the ground,

for some speech from your black muscles:

so the earth would tilt
　　under your weight,

hawks plummet upward, the dead
　　float in the air like flies,

and we, thrown from our warm furrows,
　　relearn our balance,
　　　　reach out in the dark to test

our crooked new bones.

Turnip Field

Salt comes in with the wind
off the bay: some days
the air
      is thick with it; it stirs
the roots of the tongue, unearths
and splits the husks of taste —
balsam, marsh hay, bull flanks,
      berries, greens

which fuel this green fire,
this burning off
      of the dead hair

of turnips, big as heads,
piled up on the track: meat
for swine and cattle,

plucked junk earth eyes staring
at the man in blue overalls
whose honed fork glitters
in the flame as it
turns the smouldering leaves and stalks,
his mouth full of smoke

so he doesn't taste
fir, grass, muscle, apple,
the wind thick with salt,
but only watches
the way it stirs and
whips up his fires.

The Onion

I have risen from your body
full of smoke, charred fibres;

the light kicks up off
the glazed snow: I have to
turn from its keenness,
its warmth, seeking
darkness, burying ground;

I am without grace, I cannot shape
those languages, the knots
of light and silence:
the newness of being
still, the press
of the snow's whiteness.

Young steers turned from the barn
stand, furry stones, streaked
with dung,
cold light, thin
February snow.

In this kitchen warmth I reach
for the bouquet
of thyme and sage, drifting
in the heat: a world crumbles
over my hands, I am washed
with essences;

I cup the onion I watched grow all summer:
cutting perfectly through its heart
it speaks a white core, pale
green underskin, the perfections
I have broken, that curing grace
my knife releases;

and then you are by me, unfolded
to a white stillness, remade warmth on warmth.

So we turn from our darkness,
our brokenness,
share this discovered root,
this one quiet bread
quick with light, thyme, that deep
speech of your hands which always
defeats me, calling me through strange earths
to this place suddenly yours.

Ghazal I

Now you have burned your books: you'll go
with nothing but your blind, stupefied heart.

On the hook, big trout lie like stone:
terror, and they fiercely whip their heads, unmoved.

Kitchens, women and fire: can you
do without these, your blood in your mouth?

Rough wool, oil-tanned leather, prime northern goose down,
a hard, hard eye.

Think of your house: as you speak, it falls,
fond, foolish man. And your wife.

They call it the thing of things, essence
of essences: great northern snowy owl; whiteness.

Ghazal XXXVII

Now you have burned your books, you'll go with nothing.
A heart.

The world is full of the grandeur,
and it is.

Perfection of tables: crooked grains;
and all this talk: this folly of tongues.

Too many stories: yes, and
high talk: the exact curve of the thing.

Sweetness and lies: the hook, grey deadly bait,
a wind and water to kill cedar, idle men, the innocent

not love, and hard eyes
over the cold,

not love (eyes, hands, hands, arm)
given, taken, to the marrow;

(the grand joke: *le mot juste:*
forget it; remember):

Waking is all: readiness:
you are watching;

I'll learn by going:
Sleave-silk flies; the kindly ones.

Open-Air Museum

How we stare at objects they kept
For ornament or use, clothes they put on —
Stiff, voluminous, quaint,
We cannot see ourselves in them —
Their buildings transported, re-erected,
Every numbered beam and stone correct.
We strain to see them inhabit these,
With moods like ours, passions, aims,
Whose death to them was future tense;
Now they lie, unnumbered, not for viewing,
Of lesser substance than blanched effigies
We have made assume their being.
We have installed them in these places,
None will stir to disturb the scene,
Yet how we pore over them, like usurpers
Ever anxious to secure our succession:
Each our own historian, we say
Life was slower, more gracious in their day —
Or, how lucky is our deliverance
From their dirt, inhibitions, ignorance:
The most piquant thought is their lives are done,
But our advantage is a passing one . . .

Wishful Fall

It seems everlasting, this mild delusive fall,
Gold-dusting nearest windowed hills
Of sombre spruce, bright streamered
Tamarack. The grass never green so late

Nor thick-stalked dahlias such insouciant
Budders and breakers. Yet it is all,
Like us, keen watchers of its clinging beauties,
Braced, breath-held, in downward darkness
Till that crass Victorian bridegroom,
Obliterating winter, crashes unwelcome
Up our frail stairs, bursts in upon
Our attic wishful watching, thrusts home
Yet again how pathetic our lukewarm
Economies of hope against his season.

Presence and Process

The loved being takes place
in air, whose absence
air ignores . . .
This evanescent
mystery of presence
suggests how shoots
climb, die, persist:
slight blond grasses
in corners, lee of fence,
drypoint meadowsweet,
hydrangeas'
friable clusters
against snow
though entangled in process
exact minute attention.

10 Reasons Why I Fall in Love with Inaccessible
Straight Boys Every Damn Time

1. cause when he laughs at my jokes or tells me he likes my
    clothes it can't be anything but the truth.

2. straight boys speak a foreign tongue I never learned —
    a semaphore of scruffy chin tugs, bearish shoulders, and
    dead dog easy posture. straight boys can spit, far, and
    seem to like urinals.

3. a straight boy will always hate the opera and will never,
    ever play some god-awful Whitney Houston record before
    he feels you up on the couch — straight boys like guitars.

4. cause foreign films are for girls with glasses or nervous
    Anglican boys who went to private school — and Yes, Thank
    You, he does eat meat.

5. straight boys don't trust their fathers either.

6. a straight boy will wear a tight tee-shirt no matter how fat
    he is. I call this Innocence.

7. OK, yes, even if he does have three kids and two monthly car
    payments and at least one house he still has more money than
    most of the fags I know and Money = Relaxation.

8. cause once I went to the Y and I swear to God four straight
    boys massaged each other buck-naked and talked about body
    fat ratios and not one got hard or even a little glassy
    eyed and I knew, I knew I was on a another planet and I have
    always wanted to see the stars up close.

9. straight boys remind me of children — big, hapless, grown-up children with sex organs it would be right and legal and far more interesting to touch.

10. because women don't really trust them, they'd be better off with me.

"insight into private affairs . . . raises certain barristers and magistrates to such great heights"

remember, you and I are not supposed

our bodies, little principalities
annexed   brought to heel   all our subjects, resworn

the difference between dangerous and quaint is   years under occupation

by Dad's tongue, Mom's china patterns, every teacher's
talktalktalk of man and woman   we learned
to design the master's bedrooms, kitchens, stationery, printed
sheets, hair   and clever talk

for a pittance   for a treaty signed with crossed fingers
for decriminalization
we agreed to not speak about love, early cultures, old border
disputes   every fucking thing we made for them

remember   you and I are not supposed
to betray the dubbing
but we catch our lips moving out of frame   mangling foreign
words   ugly with sincerity

Men Together

"Nature had taken pains to keep the fatal secret from us. There remains, therefore, only the extraordinary accident of some volcano."

— Jean-Jacques Rousseau

acetylene, all manner of racks, pins   the 7 poisons known only to emperors
such ineffective tortures
          to make me talk   My man, just shut up, slam my door   make like
                                                                    the wind
fast and vernal, your voice
     a hard single click of unnerving airiness
   so brittle — like the skin of firecrackers or seaweed pressed into circles —
you demand attention   (*let it come down, come down*)
and I give
peaceful man, keep me up tonight   slap me if you need

pretend it's 1946, and I need bruising, slugging, brandy chasers, a felt hat
knocked to the floor, followed by handshakes
we can be men together   (no one's watching)   we can suffer abrubt
changes of logic, bleary songs at lampposts   midnight prescriptions
(steak over the eye)   because a fire sticks to our skin   leaves
a blackened corn stink, a burnt steam, that smell plugs make after blue sparks
a fire dries our mouths to salt and oily grit, crisped hairs   leaves us
dirty and lonely as puppies

my man, my tired man   light the lights

Simone Signoret, Beldam
(for Peter Lynch)

under water, her limed hands spread   the basest ligature, each
    delects in murder and, later, another butter-white cigarette (*tabac
Maroc*, on the eve of Franz Fanon)   glints, a bright
contrary to the sneaky, fattening purples of Klieg lights, the illegal
lead in post-war cold creams   the off-colour flush of the play
                                                         murderess

you watch, think   it can't be so easy
to put a life out under the tap   to make her woman's hands grave
                                                        as rocks
as oars   to disregard the exigency of Plot

harsh and distracted, she is confident of more grey suits, more tiled
floors clicking dykish impatience   more pleated fronts and wet grass
to buff the heat between her breasts   a hundred more movies
fixated with bathtubs

later, she will publish, speak out, resist a government, bed Palestinians
(or was that Françoise Sagan?)   forget her lines, drink at breakfast
finally   snap — as only a living argument can — behind a parked
Mustang, vomiting before her 200th public defence of the auteur theory
    the hateful siren charge of patricide

Celebrity is a ticklish fabric

Rimbaud:
    "That is all in the past. Nowadays I know how to greet beauty."

                backwards Ophelia, citizeness

In Cézanne's studio, we're dappled with joy

On a dish recline the peaches. Brilliant yellow, burnt vermillion
and green earth his palette, silence in the high room.

Always they face him, waiting. He thinks light, paints
a dark cleft. Such soft cheeks. Their curves.

Like a bed the white cloth under them. Bright, silky, it rises
and falls before him, slides from the smooth table down canvas.

He opens sweet flesh. Strange glamour,
lush nakedness gazing up. Before the rich brocade curtain,

the gleaming jug. He bends over their serious faces,
discards the brush.

Claude Monet's Water Landscapes

They were his victory in old age,
seductive as Venus — strong, invisible legs,
water lily clusters pearly pink, then
mauve. They looked
at him, women in silk underclothes,
the rushing flames of alcove and bed.
Passing clouds trailed new light
over their faces. Even asleep, his eyes migrated
into their blooms. Soft rain and winds
tinged his pleasure. Waterbound muses of deep
promise, each day hosts
and guests, they rose from the mirror

of true desire, as his garden grew
ripe. No swaying or sweeping
or unlit swirls through midnight fields
disturbed their magic tête-à-tête.

December 1972: First Winter Ascension of the Sass Maor

We climbed the Sass Maor's snowy finery
Three ice-fixed December days, with the sun
Pushing a cold beam across grey rock bones
Solemn as the sheathed whiteness of a ghost.
Four climbers piercing the sky's blue glare.
Men dangling hope-ropes onto abyss-steam.
Hands nagging to be home, we were intent
Like bowed surgeons stitching a frothing wound.
And on those frost-gloved nights I dreamed
My twenty-metre fall nine years later
When the peg twisted, giving way
To hurl me into the stubborn and naked
Void; that pain-stained mouth;
Nothingness ripening under my feet.

Tattoo

After the war she could live
only *Auschwitz*, sitting with relatives
in their sunlit kitchen, her immortal
rock. And when she ate the chocolate
cake and picked up all the crumbs,
it was always *Auschwitz*, a new disbelief,

maybe, or the cell blocks now
bolted, like the soot sky,
the tiered bunks a watermark
left intact inside her head. Each sip
of coffee in the china cup,
a fresh flow of grief
she'd shouldered, had been
miraculously freed from, but now
it was everything, the dress
she pulled tight around her hips,
black comb in her hair, nephews
when they turned cartwheels,
all cast down the mass grave
of that word. And in dreams
she sang it, dark lullaby
as she strained
to wake, cradling,
her tattooed arm
like a lost child.

Dikes on Fundy Bay

Not the austere
tired stone parapets
above heavy tugboats and green canals

but the squatty, earthen parade
of dikes built by the Acadians.
Bulwarks guarding the queen's hay,
mounds brandishing goldenrod,
humped backs left from a long wrestle —

And seaward the diligent tides
polishing naked mudflats
twice a day.

ALAN R. WILSON

Antlia the Air Pump

A graduate student visits Einstein in his Princeton study.
She plies him: questions on cyclotron design, time dilation,

the bending of light by a heavy body. He answers
conscientiously, expands on every point with an example.

Her rosy bike glows next to his (indigo) in the window.
With a nod at the sun, he suggests they break for a spin.

He unclips his air pump and squeezes her tires,
explains why pressure just shy of 40 yields the easiest ride.

They mount. His speed surprises her. She pedals
hard to keep up. The cyclists accelerate past the outer

ring of buildings — coalesce into an arc of colour.
The hours wheel away (seem like minutes) as they circle,

laughing crazily, along the woodland trails, where he flips
over twice showing her how to ride without hands.

Pegasus the Winged Horse

Those final, fall evenings: my father
grappling with the fingers of disease

peeling him like a scab from the planet's face.
My uncle would hoist me with burly arms

onto his back and spirit me away
from the cries erupting through that house.

Deep into the field I rode my avuncular steed,
as the tall grass kicked at my feet, as the failing light

pulled us slowly from the ground.
Stopped for air, he would run a forefinger along

the constellations: the ones he invented on the spot,
the ones my father and he learned from their father:

Andromeda chained to a rock, mighty Pegasus
bearing the abyss of space on white shoulders.

Octans the Octant

> *No stellar domain can match Octans, at the south*
> *celestial pole, for barrenness and poverty of stars.*
> — The Heavens

The highways of Antarctica blow constantly
with snow: speeding drifts fuelled by the gales

which cruise the icy lanes of the continent.
There are no towns, no destinations, nothing to connect

but the snow and wind and long cold of the year's
single night. Yet sometimes gas pumps appear

like white-hooded figures, and behind, a diner
with nobody there, glittering in the blue of a swaying light.

There are also stories spread by the wind

of ghostly machines crossing the landscape in threes,

the polar night snapping, howling at their ploughs,
of chilled shapes and pale, pale hands

that navigate the storms with only
rumours of a north star to guide them.

Lynx
(for Anne)

If I am first in the ground, visit me,
Even if snow lies deep on that cold hill.

Forget the cut flowers. Forget the chill.
Your toasty arrangement of toes will be

My bouquet. And no burial decree
Will seal our separation — a few still

Feet below yours lies the man who, until
He hugged the soil, loved you exclusively.

Despite the desolation of the snow,
The deer shall pass like ghosts through the gravestones.

The bear shall heat his resting place. Above,
The lynx shall watch you through the icy glow

Of bare branches, like the stubborn thoughts of
A man who still sees you through his own bones.

NOVA SCOTIA

A Basement Tale
(for Andrew)

1

Twin brothers slept on thin cots near a furnace.
One heard a gruff lullaby, a fiery-hearted father;
the other, a smoky-fingered devil sharpening a blade.

With a click and a shudder, the furnace shut off.
For one boy, silence was a shoreless pool rippled
by a single minnow; for the other, a spider,
the tips of eight legs pressed against his face.

Rain slapped the basement windows and seeped in
through cracks — the sky at work feeding rhubarb
in the back yard; the slow growth of mould
over split stones in a Loyalist burial ground.

When the bathroom fan overhead whirred, one brother
heard a whale, fathoms deep, serenading its mate;
the other, an open-mouthed ghost trapped in an iceberg.

2

A click, a shudder — the droning began again.
The twins crawled from bed and slept in the furnace.

One walked into a tropical forest hung heavy with fruit,
shot through with birds spanning the spectrum;
one fell into an inferno that burned up his clothes
and glasses, his eyelashes and lips.

Each brother wrote a book — one with berry juice
and feathers, one with his finger stone-slashed.

3

Upstairs the next day they read each other's words,
baffled. Baffled, curled in back-to-back chairs,
they knit their brows into mazes without threads.

That midnight, back on their hands and knees
they crawled down a trail toward each other's dream
from the crossroads inside the blazing mouth.

Always

Somewhere a wolf spider dances on a white rock
shaking in fervent frenzy. Somewhere a crippled auk
tries to fly, kildeer mate in a soccer field, a shrike
shoves a warbler onto a thorn. At this moment
a woman watches a meteor, a child counts the seconds
between lightning and thunder, old men share
ale made from malt, hops, and Scottish water.
Always, during your day and during your night
blackflies pierce human skin, rice-shoots
poke through earth, worms tunnel, a mother grazes
her infant's cheek with love for the first time.
Always, heat at the heart of a crematorium is reaching
its peak, and a queen bee drops dead into mud. Pick
any moment: a couple on a mountain inhale air too thin
for their lungs, but feel inexplicably at home,
while a couple wandering through their garden
catch the smells of two dozen species, feel lifted
into an exotic place. Now, as I write, rain cascades
into a shrunken stream, foxes nip each other,
a rotting peach loses its last firmness. As you read,
a skirt falls to a bedroom floor, tires crush
a crawling animal, fingers press piano keys.

What happens during a pause in your talk
could keep you typing until your last breath. Always
a bullet leaves a gun, honey pours from a spoon.
Your brain is a mussel shell that will never hold the ocean.

from *Talking to the Birds*

2. *to a northern gannet*

Fog like cold sweat coated every inch of the ferry,
swathed and hid the ocean ten feet out. Downstairs
indoors, passengers snacked, napped,
fought the warriors and demons of video games.

For those of us circling the deck
the first hour of the crossing didn't yield
one bird, one mewl or wayward cry. Grand Manan
could've been a mile off, or a thousand.
If allowed extravagance, I'd say
the waves peaked and toppled like the waves
                        in the story of the seven days
when "everything according to its kind"
was born. Then, you:
                        flying, unmistakable, goose-sized,
your butter-yellow head the one contrast
to all that pallor. Where everything else was wispy
and smudged, you were suddenness, otherness,
completeness,
eyes and beak and wingbeat.

Just as quickly, you slipped back behind
the gathering of spectres. When I pushed closer
against the cold iron railing
                        you were back with me,

then vanished again, like a feeling that keeps coming
and going on the verge of sleep.
For a minute you were the first bird, or the last.

The Afterlife of Trees
(for Don McKay)

Neither sheep nor cows crisscross our lives as much.
Trees dangle apples and nuts for the hungry, throw
shade down for lovers, mark sites for the lost,
and first and last are
utterly themselves,
fuller and finer than any letter or number,
any 7 or T. Their fragmentary afterlife goes on
in a guitar's body and a hockey stick, in the beaked faces
up a totem pole and the stake through a vampire's heart,
in a fragrant cheeseboard, a Welsh love-spoon,
a sweat-stained axe handle, a giant green dragonfly
suspended from the ceiling with twine,
in the spellbinding shapechanging
behind a glass woodstove door . . .

and in a table I sanded and finished this week.
— *Finished?* — Four grades of sandpaper drew out
alder's "nature," inimitable amoeba shapes,
waves, half moons, paw prints dissolving in mud.
What looks more beautiful after death? We sand
and sand, but under the stain, beyond our pottery
and books, our fallen hairs trapped in the varnish,
something remains like memories of a buck
rubbing its horns on bark. Soaked in
deeper than the grain goes: cries, whistles, hoots.

At the Fishhouses

Although it is a cold evening,
down by one of the fishhouses
an old man sits netting,
his net, in the gloaming almost invisible,
a dark purple-brown,
and his shuttle worn and polished.
The air smells so strong of codfish
it makes one's nose run and one's eyes water.
The five fishhouses have steeply peaked roofs
and narrow, cleated gangplanks slant up
to storerooms in the gables
for the wheelbarrows to be pushed up and down on.
All is silver: the heavy surface of the sea,
swelling slowly as if considering spilling over,
is opaque, but the silver of the benches,
the lobster pots, and masts, scattered
among the wild jagged rocks,
is of an apparent translucence
like the small old buildings with an emerald moss
growing on their shoreward walls.
The big fish tubs are completely lined
with layers of beautiful herring scales
and the wheelbarrows are similarly plastered
with creamy iridescent coats of mail,
with small iridescent flies crawling on them.
Up on the little slope behind the houses,
set in the sparse bright sprinkle of grass,
is an ancient wooden capstan,
cracked, with two long bleached handles
and some melancholy stains, like dried blood,
where the ironwork has rusted.
The old man accepts a Lucky Strike.
He was a friend of my grandfather.
We talk of the decline in the population

and of codfish and herring
while he waits for a herring boat to come in.
There are sequins on his vest and on his thumb.
He has scraped the scales, the principal beauty,
from unnumbered fish with that black old knife,
the blade of which is almost worn away.

Down at the water's edge, at the place
where they haul up the boats, up the long ramp
descending into the water, thin silver
tree trunks are laid horizontally
across the grey stones, down and down
at intervals of four or five feet.

Cold dark deep and absolutely clear,
element bearable to no mortal,
to fish and to seals . . . One seal particularly
I have seen here evening after evening.
He was curious about me. He was interested in music;
like me a believer in total immersion,
so I used to sing him Baptist hymns.
I also sang "A Mighty Fortress Is Our God."
He stood up in the water and regarded me
steadily, moving his head a little.
Then he would disappear, then suddenly emerge
almost in the same spot, with a sort of shrug
as if it were against his better judgement.
Cold dark deep and absolutely clear,
the clear grey icy water . . . Back, behind us,
the dignified tall firs begin.
Bluish, associating with their shadows,
a million Christmas trees stand
waiting for Christmas. The water seems suspended
above the rounded grey and blue-grey stones.
I have seen it over and over, the same sea, the same,
slightly, indifferently swinging above the stones,
icily free above the stones,
above the stones and then the world.
If you should dip your hand in,

your wrist would ache immediately,
your bones would begin to ache and your hand would burn
as if the water were a transmutation of fire
that feeds on stones and burns with a dark grey flame.
If you tasted it, it would first taste bitter,
then briny, then surely burn your tongue.
It is like what we imagine knowledge to be:
dark, salt, clear, moving, utterly free,
drawn from the cold hard mouth
of the world, derived from the rocky breasts
forever, flowing and drawn, and since
our knowledge is historical, flowing, and flown.

Cape Breton

Out on the high "bird islands," Ciboux and Hertford,
the razorbill auks and the silly-looking puffins all stand
with their backs to the mainland
in solemn, uneven lines along the cliff's brown grass-frayed edge,
while the few sheep pastured there go "Baaa, baaa."
(Sometimes, frightened by aeroplanes, they stampede
and fall over into the sea or onto the rocks.)
The silken water is weaving and weaving,
disappearing under the mist equally in all directions,
lifted and penetrated now and then
by one shag's dripping serpent-neck,
and somewhere the mist incorporates the pulse,
rapid but unurgent, of a motorboat.

The same mist hangs in thin layers
among the valleys and gorges of the mainland
like rotting snow-ice sucked away
almost to spirit; the ghosts of glaciers drift
among those folds and folds of fir: spruce and hackmatack —

dull, dead, deep peacock-colours,
each riser distinguished from the next
by an irregular nervous saw-tooth edge,
alike, but certain as a stereoscopic view.

The wild road clambers along the brink of the coast.
On it stand occasional small yellow bulldozers,
but without their drivers, because today is Sunday.
The little white churches have been dropped into the matted hills
like lost quartz arrowheads.
The road appears to have been abandoned.
Whatever the landscape had of meaning appears to have been
    abandoned,
unless the road is holding it back, in the interior,
where we cannot see,
where deep lakes are reputed to be,
and disused trails and mountains of rock
and miles of burnt forests standing in grey scratches
like the admirable scriptures made on stones by stones —
and these regions now have little to say for themselves
except in thousands of light song-sparrow songs floating upward
freely, dispassionately, through the mist, and meshing
in brown-wet, fine, torn fishnets.

A small bus comes along, in up-and-down rushes,
packed with people, even to its step.
(On weekdays with groceries, spare automobile parts, and pump
    parts,
but today only two preachers extra, one carrying his frock coat on a
    hanger.)
It passes the closed roadside stand, the closed schoolhouse,
where today no flag is flying
from the rough-adzed pole topped with a white china doorknob.
It stops, and a man carrying a baby gets off,
climbs over a stile, and goes down through a small steep meadow,
which establishes its poverty in a snowfall of daisies,
to his invisible house beside the water.

The birds keep on singing, a calf bawls, the bus starts.
The thin mist follows
the white mutations of its dream;
an ancient chill is rippling the dark brooks.

Poem

About the size of an old-style dollar bill,
American or Canadian,
mostly the same whites, grey greens, and steel greys
— this little painting (a sketch for a larger one?)
has never earned any money in its life.
Useless and free, it has spent seventy years
as a minor family relic
handed along collaterally to owners
who looked at it sometimes, or didn't bother to.

It must be Nova Scotia; only there
does one see gabled wooden houses
painted that awful shade of brown.
The other houses, the bits that show, are white.
Elm trees, low hills, a thin church steeple
— that grey-blue wisp — or is it? In the foreground
a water meadow with some tiny cows,
two brush strokes each, confidently cows;
two minuscule white geese in the blue water,
back-to-back, feeding, and a slanting stick.
Up closer, a wild iris, white and yellow,
fresh-squiggled from the tube.
The air is fresh and cold; cold early spring
clear as grey glass; a half inch of blue sky
below the steel-grey storm clouds.
(They were the artist's speciality.)
A specklike bird is flying to the left.
Or is it a flyspeck looking like a bird?

Heavens, I recognize the place, I know it!
It's behind — I can almost remember the farmer's name.
His barn backed on that meadow. There it is,
titanium white, one dab. The hint of steeple,
filaments of brush hairs, barely there,
must be the Presbyterian church.
Would that be Miss Gillespie's house?
Those particular geese and cows
are naturally before my time.

A sketch done in an hour, "in one breath,"
once taken from a trunk and handed over.
Would you like this? I'll probably never
have room to hang these things again.
Your Uncle George, no, mine, my Uncle George,
he'd be your great-uncle, left them all with Mother
when he went back to England.
You know, he was quite famous, an R.A. . . .

I never knew him. We both knew this place,
apparently, this literal small backwater,
looked at it long enough to memorize it,
our years apart. How strange. And it's still loved,
or its memory is (it must have changed a lot).
Our visions coincided — "visions" is
too serious a word — our looks, two looks:
art "copying from life" and life itself,
life and the memory of it so compressed
they've turned into each other. Which is which?
Life and the memory of it cramped,
dim, on a piece of Bristol board,
dim, but how live, how touching in detail
— the little that we get for free,
the little of our earthly trust. Not much.
About the size of our abidance
along with theirs: the munching cows,
the iris, crisp and shivering, the water
still standing from spring freshets,
the yet-to-be-dismantled elms, the geese.

Nova Scotia Fish Hut

Rain, and blown sand, and southwest wind
Have rubbed these shingles crisp and paper-thin.
Come in:
Something has stripped these studding-posts and pinned
Time to the rafters. Where the woodworm ticked
Shick shick shick shick
Steady and secretive, his track is plain:
The fallen bark is dust; the beams are bare.

Bare as the bare stone of this open shore,
This building grey as stone. The filtered sun
Leaks cold and quiet through it. And the rain,
The wind, the whispering sand, return to finger
Its creaking wall, and creak its thuttering door.

Old, as the shore is. But they use the place.
Wait if you like: someone will come to find
A handline or gutting knife, or stow
A coiled net in the loft. Or just to smoke
And loaf; and swap tomorrow in slow talk;
And knock his pipe out on a killick-rock
Someone left lying sixty years ago.

Early Morning Landing

In daylight, there is life and living speech;
The constant grumble, the resilient splash
Of slow tide lifting on a slanted beach;
And blowing sunlight. And the measured flash

Of the sea marching . . . But the beach and bay
Are vague as midnight now; in midnight thinned
At the sky's edge by the first hint of grey.
And calm as sleep before the morning wind.

Calmer than sleep. But the eyes lift to find
In the veiled night the faint recurring spark
Of a known beacon. And the listening mind
Wakes in the stillness; and the veil is stirred
By a dim ghost of sound — a far-off word
And the soft thump of rowlocks in the dark.

Orchard in the Woods

Red spruce and fir have crossed the broken lines
Where ragged fences ran; ground juniper
Covers the sunny slope where currant bushes
Blackened their hanging clusters in green leaves.
Where oats and timothy moved like leaning water
Under the cloudy sweep of August wind,
The crop is stunted alders and tall ferns.

Above the cellar's crust of falling stone
Where timbered walls endured the treacherous
Traffic of frost and sunlight, nothing stands . . .
Under the wreckage of the vanished barn
A woodchuck burrows. Where the dooryard was,
The matted grass of years encloses now
Two horseshoes and a rusted wagon tire.

Only the apple trees recall the dream
That flowered here — in love and sweat and growth,
Anger and longing. Tough and dark and wild,
Grown big of stump, rough in the bark and old,

They still put forth a light ironic bloom
Against the green utility of spruce.

Clearing and field and buildings gone to waste —
But in the fall, a gunner going home
Will halt a moment, lift a hand to reach
One dusky branch above the crooked track,
And, thinking idly of his kitchen fire,
Bite to the small black shining seeds and learn
The taste of ninety seasons, hard and sweet.

GEORGE ELLIOTT CLARKE

Blank Sonnet

The air smells of rhubarb, occasional
Roses, or first birth of blossoms, a fresh,
Undulant hurt, so body snaps and curls
Like flower. I step through snow as thin as script,
Watch white stars spin dizzy as drunks, and yearn
To sleep beneath a patchwork quilt of rum.
I want the slow, sure collapse of language
Washed out by alcohol. Lovely Shelley,
I have no use for measured, cadenced verse
If you won't read. Icarus-like, I'll fall
Against this page of snow, tumble blackly
Across vision to drown in the white sea
That closes every poem — the white reverse
That cancels the blackness of each image.

Haligonian Market Cry

I got hallelujah watermelons! — virginal pears! — virtuous corn!
Munit haec et altera vincit!
Luscious, fat-ass watermelons! — plump pears! — big-butt corn!
Le gusta este jardin?
Come-and-get-it cucumbers — hot-to-trot, lust-fresh cucumbers!
Voulez-vous coucher avec moi?
Watermelons! — Go-to-church-and-get-redeemed watermelons!
O peccatore, in verità!
Good God cucumbers! — righteous pears! — golden Baptist corn!
Die Reue ist doch nur ein leuchter Kauf!
I got sluttish watermelons! — sinful cucumbers! — jail-bait pears! —
Planted by Big-Mouth Chaucer and picked by Evil Shakespeare!

Blue Elegies: I. v

October, Gothic October: no lovers loiter, lounge,
in Annapolis Royal's "Historic Gardens."
Naturally: Love poems wither in our bleak, stony,
frigid, hostile, brutal Canuck anthologies.
Maybe all hardy Canadian poetry erupts lavishly
from some solitary, sullen naturalist's notebook.
See! A last bee, still stockpiling pollen, hums hotly
against this Octobral creep of cold. Octopoid
　　networks and wires of downed branches and briars
and twigs, prickling and muddling and needling, obscure
　　a scrappy bit of light, famished, gorging on a slice
of brown-black, brackish, leaf-plastered
　　subsidiary pond, wafting orange-green-brown lily pads
and a certain tangy tart stink —
　　maybe of algae and oak leaves, decaying,
and the *bizz* of wispy, final, waifish insects.
Everything here is allegory for allegations.
Look! The dyked marsh is sucking, slurping, the Fundy —
　　the tall, hay-like grass, hay-smelling, springs
out of rank black mud, crabby, with fronds and fringes of muck,
　　then sodden, mud-coralled water giving back
a sky of grey-and-white-peppered clouds, blue shards also,
　　conjoining dark evergreen spikes,
grey, ghostly, scrawny things, or gold or gold-orange sprays
　　and tufts the colour of a blonde *fillette*.
Nearby accumulates a pungent cascade of leaves,
　　then the thick, gigantic stalks of marsh grass,
with sunlight baying in — nostalgic, regretful, imploring —
　　like the speaker in a John Thompson *ghazal*,
with the last maniacal mosquitoes, whining, *comme des pleûtres*,
　　and strafing still-fragrant, still-bloody roses,
near where the train tracks are *kaput*, all torn up now,
　　these roses glistening and perfuming dogmatically
while the eye hooks on notorious, flagrant, orange-red trees
　　and bowers of vines, other overhanging things,
darkening, just as the sun darkens while first launching light

against the dykes, the marsh, in dying brilliance
equivalent to what Carman paints in "Low Tide at Grand Pré."
   Dismissive of our idiot anxieties and ironies,
stately lances the august, sepulchral, elegiac light.

Love Poem / Song Regarding Weymouth Falls

   At the *Six-Hiboux*, where the Acadian
and the Micmac saw the six scholar-birds
whose insomnia is natural,
probably a million moons ago;
at the Sissiboo River, where it kisses
wetly Saint Mary's Bay and fans on out
into brown Fundy tides shimmering
like a new world Nile;
this is where the world as we know it begins,
all blue and beguiling,
all because of her who homes with the pines,
so elegant, evergreen, egalitarian —
richly female. . . .
   At the homeless highway, where it waits
and wails asphalt anthems of hit-and-run
before plunging wildly into woods whispering
Kejimkujik songs of she I love in blossom notes
of the most crimson and pleasant apples
and the fattest calves of the land,
there is built Weymouth Falls
and its African Baptist church
and its antique lumberyard
and the dwelling of her I take time
to make time with . . .
   Ah, delirious delight is mine! — the careless
debauchery of stars bearing only good luck/

glad tidings; the sweet desolation of distance,
ebbing and flowing; drunken joy
of violent youth, violently in love,
as she moves to apex of my cosmos;
and the old, troubled world wheels around her,
song pours itself through my flesh,
drives me to her gravity-field of beauty,
even to the edge of the Sissiboo,
hand-in-hand with her.

Chopping Wood

> *Poetry is an island that breaks away from the main.*
> — Derek Walcott

All summer listening for the crack
that sounds a breach along the grain
and splits logs clean: the tone-deaf strain-
ing after perfect pitch and hack-

ing through the wood. I found the stumps
out back: discarded Ogres, Hundred-
Handed Ones (giants who thundered
once at the throne of Cronos). Clumps

of knots with fungus barnacles,
they'd sat for two years water-logged
and rotting 'til their cores were clogged
like miners' lungs. Bark had curled

away and crumbled into dust.
As ugly as the shack I'd come
to stay in: a last resort some-
where up a tidal river just

east of a peninsular,
provincial border — Tidnish Bridge
in Nova Scotia: on the edge
of forests breathing in salt air.

Although the blade was sharp, at night
I had to soak the shaft to swell
the wood and keep the axhead still,
the stumps being strung with knots so tight

my strokes just stunned the loosening tool.
I hearkened after rhythms in
the timber's pitch accustoming
themselves to my accent's iron rule.

Instead, those blunt caesuras in
the wood: the axhead buried to
the hilt in stumps to worry you
with legends meant for measuring

that one true strength. More often logs
disintegrated into sticks
for kindling and the scattered chips
of lumbering's poor epilogues.

Or, when the stroke was followed through
for once, and blocks would fall from stress
and burden on the stumps, I'd cleft
honeycomb-hollowed slews

of ant nests spilling insects heads
and eggs among the bits of wood:
small rural slaughters for the good
of keeping strangers warm in bed?

I spent midsummer living in
a shack, listening to hacked wood scold;
a chopped cord stored against the cold
though none would be there shivering.

Watermarks

The sun-beat, salt-scrubbed, sooty wooden boards
that run like foolscap up the walls of homes,
taking to heart Time's taste for monochromes,
are all washed out from facing up to fog;
the chalk-stained slate of their wrinkled scowl
is what remains of lifetimes staring down
the local climate and the smokestacks' smog.

Among the walls of solid, happy colours
that splash the steep hill stepping from the harbour
(as if a giant child had dropped his building blocks),
these plain-faced homes, like a shoreline's watermarks,
will bear as level-headed witness as
horizons, so long as such perspectives last.
Not that their posture's one to emulate:
they pitch and lean like old men getting slow-
ly drunk alone in Legions, like woodpiles left
as a wood's libation, breakers about to crash;
but *on the level*, having seen too much
to strike at anything you'd call a pose.

Once sailors' rooms, they seem to imitate
the ocean's frown — that grey brow creased by waves —
or ruled but empty pages in a log
that's been abandoned, scattered looseleaf sheets
I've tried to gather in a manuscript.
With nothing else to give to make up for
so many years away, nothing to
repay a landscape for the beauty laid
across a childhood like a crazy quilt,
may my words lie down on pages as
mariners may have lain on bunkhouse beds:
exhausted and grateful.
                    And if these clapboard shacks
have nothing against the seasons printing them

as fading background in a local woodcut,
let them then not mind these offset lines
so much themselves like wooden siding or
irregularly breaking rows of waves.
At best, a poem's just one more bank of pass-
ing fog for them; or perhaps a rising tide
that always falls again, so fast, so fast.

Lorne, Nova Scotia
   (for M.M.)

Millstones rest their weathered bulk
against a glazed lawn;
half-buried, they look,
with one bored eye apiece, long

past visitors to this house.
His mill collapsed
some time before he cursed
and took his final steps.

Now his body's beyond mend
in some hospital bed.
Only the belligerent
tongue of his sunken head

worries the air.
Swaddled: his sheets as still
as the huge space of winter
weighing on the mill.

The dam in a caul of ice,
shushing the fall

of water underneath;
the bull-chain pulls

apart, the headsaw's seized.
Still down on the farm,
her life seems
undone. In the barn

tools blur with rust
into thin air.
In the house
wooden furniture

shines, not with polish,
but decades of use —
the set and shift of muscles,
the body's only truth.

Time, in winter,
passes mostly in the dark.
Her bones are curling her
into a question mark.

Banns

these birds are all the wedding dresses of the world
these trees all the brides waiting

you can begin no journey here without marriage

when I arrived I knew the shadow
would be long and hard to follow
shadow of a matchmaker stretching thinly through the grass
but I came to walk here
to marry the heartbeats that collect
on birch leaves after rain has fallen
the minute ones without home or chest in which to beat
without blood to send pouring through the silence

I love what can't be seen   I marry what can't be seen
and so walk through the forest via homages
the invisible knowing of no hand that it hasn't held
no hand without a wedding ring like a quiet storm
moving round a finger
shy gold that carries every moment darkened on currents
studies of one flesh
every bird in the air.

Child of the Earth

1

at evening the musk of falling snow reaches the earth
snow that will fall all night   turning round in pivots of space
spaces centred on moonlight   the moonlit ridges
of the self that abounds

so many selves make up the nightly routines   so many
fall with the snow upon the land   drown in the wintry sea

the body sits and the snow drifts down at light's end
the self drifts into woods and hills
arriving long after the world was made
the dark somewheres already in place and folded
as if time had passed   folded as you suppose it would be
if you arrived late to sit alone among the trees
among the cool embraces   the awayness of snow.

2

sitting in the woods you think of other worlds
planets where snow also falls   sulphur snows   iodine snows
the arsenic snows of Saturn   neptunium snows
toothed hills filling with empurpled flakes of neon
this great depth of distances is comforting
among pine trees who have no inheritors but themselves
beside the river frozen to a strength
that would break if it moved
and you think of things that you can't bear without shadows
leaning in upon your flesh   all the semblances leaning there.

3

snow heals the moment's burn
which is bright as Alpha Cygnus
of fixed position   of infinite birth
of indissoluble address
heals the wound that secretes its appetite upon you
knives that shave solace below the flesh

you sit as snow drops past the meridian
past the cuffs of trees
down among the inscrutable levels
to atoms forgetting reality
to a bare place where all visible things appear
as shades if they appear at all
ghosting around the emptiness
calling the elements home to their beds
home to every harm left unattended
a winter that surrounds you   seeable among the trees.

4

for many lifetimes the snow fell and you were the stillness
positioned there
you were the mechanics of snow and twisted ends of stars
structures of the self growing and fading into birth

O child of the earth you are me and us and the rabbit
who has believed longer than we have   purling evocations
in his warren like blood moving through its tunnels
seeking the backs of our legs   the palms of our hands
the movement it feasts upon   the edible motion

you're the pond pushing life out from its centre
cord grass drunk along the shore   bees pouring out of amber
all this which is part of the self   the cool of the night
the fire behind us we rarely see   quietude
you're the ocean setting forth   the first stone it touches

the wind that will blow the snow away
blow your particles into empty space   O empty space
this is the self   all worlds   the single place.

Drowning Water

1

the cormorant carries the universe
it's a place small enough for a bird to carry

on its back the countryside tilts down to the sea
beneath its feathers a well runs deeply down into its body

you haul water up in a tin bucket
the water isn't red like cormorant's blood
but clear like the skill of drinking from your palms
folded   holding an invisible cup   you drink the cup
and unfold your hands reaching for the water again.

2

you take the water indoors   it enters a room trembling
it enters a house afraid even though its been there before
even though its been in the belly of a whale   in a teapot
in the eyes of Seneca   in a shot glass   in a glacier
even though it's passed through sewers and aquariums
been under Phoenician ships and in the stems of roses
in the wings of locust rising from a decision in the dark

it enters the house shivering as if it were cold
even though it has been mixed with blood   with soup
with earth   with food dyes that have made it bluer

than blue ever wanted to be   even though Lao-Tzu
slept with it beneath his tongue   calling it a flame
even though it has rested in the warmth of countless
breasts awaiting the child foretold by emptiness
although each time the infant is only water and morning
the ocean come back from death   laying down its head.

3

at every moment water is finished with itself   complete
with memories   with motion   with resting-places
but because of you it begins again to move the hours
into position   it picks you up once again from sleep

all day it will protect you from thirst   which is the voice
of the enemy in your throat longing to speak   to curse
the wisdom of the elements   the raindrop's preeminence
over humanity   the rapture in the plumbing
ecstasy in the kettle   the exaltation in the cloud

you who are so graceless   drowning water with your gestures
understand its patience   its tender stillness in a bowl
its true life is a silence that is always present
the faraway in an animal's mouth   the dowry of a bride unborn

you who are so unconscious   so wet with thought   know
when you leave it will wait for you   wait years for you
to return   then it will be a name to remember when you open
the door   water   a name for your name to return to.

The True Names of Birds

There are more ways to abandon a child
than to leave them at the mouth of the woods.
Sometimes by the time you find them, they've made up names
for all the birds and constellations, and they've broken
their reflections in the lake with sticks.

With my daughter came promises and vows
that unfolded through time like a roadmap and led me
to myself as a child, filled with wonder for my father
who could make sound from a wide blade of grass

and his breath. Here in the stillness of forest,
the sun columning before me temple-ancient,
that wonder is what I regret losing most; that wonder
and the true names of birds.

The moon on Friday night

                                        erased all paths to Saturday
and swept up footsteps from the day before. It coaxed buttons
to the lips of buttonholes and whispered, "you're beautiful,
so beautiful," to women who speak the vernacular

of loneliness. Softly it slid into the hands of the men
they were with and lent its light to everything they touched.
"See," the moonlight seemed to say, "there are so many ways
to be naked and so many ways to be far

from home." The light reminded the women of songs
they knew, songs written to gauge distance. Later,
still later on this island of Friday night, they sang
those songs under their breath as they bent

to tie their shoes. And they stayed bent long after
their shoes were tied, hearing the wind for the first time
caught in a bucket of baby teeth. It was then they remembered
they were toothfairies, medicine men, and their children's

mouths were empty. They knew of light switches, window
blinds, they knew to throw sand on fire, to blow
at a candle, but this light, this light they knew nothing
about so they carried it home with them. And now they wish

they hadn't. It lights up corners they'd kept dark, lights
their words and gives them new meaning. At night,
they hold their husbands' hands to their mouths.
"Know this light," they pray, "touch me with this light."

The Peonies

The peonies hold so much rain, they've collapsed
to the ground. I spent the day tying their stalks
to wooden stakes I hammered into the garden. Still

they're listless, bobbing in my arms exhausted
from blooming so long and so heavy. I leave them bent
and sweep their petals from the walkway. For days

I don't think of them. The poppies need weeding, the squash
should be thinned. And I don't think of them again until my mother
visits. It's while she talks that I'm reminded. She has that look

of peonies, her voice that weight of rain. And between us
is a walkway, cleared of all we've given, of all we've lost,
where each stone is connected in a constellation,

mother, daughter, gardener. For this moment
we are the same, we are equal. Then something
slips from her grasp and gently nestles in my arms.

On Building a Nest
St. Peter's, Saskatchewan

You've hooked up fish line and a sinker
to your light switch so you don't have to leave
your bed. One pull and
darkness. Pull it. And now
think of the broken mirror
words, the ones that hold seven years'
bad luck and shards of light
that cut. You must swallow

these words. Here's a tip:
some birds eat gravel along with seed:
the process of grinding. Here's another:
if you need to know more about luck,
study bones, the clavicle, also known as
wishbone, and its muscles that unfurl the wings.
Stop here if you already think you can fly.

Those kinds of thoughts are stones
and you'll end up going nowhere with them.
But if you've ever been walking a road and realized
roads are just another species

of longing, we should meet, outside,
at midnight: I'll be the one wearing blue. I can't promise
miracles; these things take time. Turn the light
back on. I forgot to say
you have to spend at least one week with cows. Notice how they perch
on the very edge of land
and sky. There are many birds who over the years
have lost their wings. This has nothing to do with luck
but with need, you'll see that in their eyes. And then you must crawl
into the word extinction. This word is a small cave shaped like an egg.
Your knees will be under your chin, your arms around them;
you'll have only yourself to hold onto. Here's another tip: bring
     something
to think about; you'll be there for a while. And this is important
to remember: a sparrow can sing as many as twenty variations
of the same song and a morning can have a wingspread

as wide as a week. Trees migrate from season to season
using cloud patterns and stars as guideposts. You'll have to
improvise. I'm only telling you because I'm lonely.
I've made you a shelter of twigs and this, I hope, is bright
and shiny enough to lure you in. I've been measuring
rainfall, the light of day; we're running out of time. Tomorrow
I'll sing another variation of this. Already I know it'll have something
     to do
with the word pelican
and with glide.

Passamaquoddy Song of the Stars

We are the stars that sing
We sing with our light.
We are the birds of fire,
We fly over the sky,
Our light is a voice
We make a road for spirits
For the sktekmush to pass over.

Among us are three hunters
Who chase a bear.
There never was a time
When they were not hunting.
We look down on the mountains.
This is the song of the stars.

sktekmush — spirits

You, I, Love, Beauty, Earth

Supposing you were I and I were you
You gave, I received

You would think in terms of love
Giving without thought of payment
The words of a culture
To spread and mend

Supposing I were you
And received without question

The words of a culture
Spreading news like yours

With so little, we share
But not so much of my life do you bear
Let us trade places just this once
And you listen while I go on about my culture
Important just like yours
But almost dead

Old Stories

There are stories told by the elderly
Of bannock baked in a bed of stone
Of birchbark fashioned into a pot
To boil meat and bone

There are tales told
Of what life was before
Of wigwam in the wood
With deerskin for a door

Fishing from canoe
Hunting in the wild
Herbs gathered for the sick
To cure and soothe

Prayers and song
Memories told to the young
When all life was lnua'kis

It will never be the same again
Only in our minds and elderly tales

lnua'kis — Indian

Plawej ans L'nui'site'w
(Partridge and Indian-Speaking Priest)

Once there was an Indian-speaking priest
Who learned Mi'kmaw from his flock.
He spoke the language the best he knew how
But sometimes got stuck.
They called him L'nui'site'w out of respect to him
And loving the man, he meant a lot to them.
At specific times he heard their confessions
They followed the rules, walking to the little church.
A widow woman was strolling through the village
On her way there, when one hunter gave her a day-old plawej
She took the partridge, putting it inside her coat
Thanking the couple, going her way.
At confession, the priest asked, "What is the smell?"
In Mi'kmaw she said, "My plawej."
He gave blessing and sent her on her way.
The next day he gave a long sermon, ending with the words
"Keep up the good lives you are leading,
                    but wash your plawejk."
The women giggled, he never knew why.
To this day there is a saying, they laugh and cry.
Whatever you do, wherever you go
Always wash your plawejk.

Prayer

Every hour I am disappearing
where sun collides with icy leaves
and hovers in the brilliant air.
Trees light with a backdrop of winter.
Yellow grass smoulders under leaves.
I am being translated, painstakingly,
atom by atom, into everything that breathes.
Each winter I'm present —
the earth in vestments, a white sleeve
covering its bones. Do not disturb me.
I am walking deeper into the day
where sun slips between houses.
Wind leans into me as I lean against houses.
Soon night will cast off its thin clothes
and nestle down on earth as if earth
were a blanket, the evening deep in vespers,
the smell of moss, its green incantation.
Each hour relinquishes more light.
Soon the moon will rise and make its way forward
in this dark water, this intimacy
of quiet. It's as if the door were open and I,
resonant and indecipherable as evening,
were passing through.

Scanning an Afternoon in Winter

Earth is a cipher. I read
the ocean: light, dark. Dark
that feeds light running down

the wave's smooth mouth. Trough filled
with a slough of brown. Underbelly
rising. Then, rough as bark,
a spill of foam on shore. What?
Green weeds on sand in winter? This language
dragged up from the ocean floor. Waves swell
then collapse, their lapping sound repeating,
sibilant: whish, an*guish* . . .
Sun retreats behind a thick lens then makes its way
down, the earth's belly hard.
If there's something I need to know —
earth, foam, water — *let* me know.
This inviolability floats
like ice on water in snow.

Through a Slit in the Tent

1. The woman walking turns her head
        as the car slows down. A man digging
    in a field stops to watch her,
        skirt blowing against her leg. *Woman*. Even the sound
    is private. A lake too black
        to see into. But the word itself is
    rust red, the colour of barns, or maroon, an old house
        at the end of the road, the porch light on. Inside it's dark
    the woman who lives there has gone out,
        perhaps to the water. Night beats against her
    empty door, as the man who's passing
        feels his heart beating faster. He knows
    this woman, remembers, last time,
        how she looked at him.

2. Another time
        the man lies, restless. Night enters
his sleeping bag. Through a slit
        in the tent he sees stars touching each other. Out there
a black hole in the galaxy pools with light. A summer night
        arches against it. There's a smell of salt
as when the wind is in from the sea.
        The night is narrow. Beside him the woman
moves her leg. He wants
        to touch her. He wants
"to find Venus in a diagram of the female anatomy." Even the pull
        of the earth around the sun, he thinks,
has to do with those times, late, late,
        when a man enters a woman.

3. In tents of sleep a woman
        stirs, giving the man the feeling
he is in the dream she is having. The wind
        that touches her shoulder
brushes his mouth. Night fingers
        the shells by the water. This is what brings
the sky to the ground and makes night slide
        onto the sand. Outside the tent, a glissando of water
moistens a deep, splayed channel. A bud
        presses against a leaf.
A woman *evokes* . . . No.
        A woman *reveals* . . . No.
The sky is down on its knees
        giving up all the rain inside it.

This is a story that begins at the end.
You have to walk slowly back (as the man will do)
in the dark. The woman inside the tent stretches her legs
as the first curve of light softens the eastern sky.

The Sadness of Windows

They shoulder each other in old houses, these windows,
catch light as it fades
and store a glint that draws us in.
Behind this we house our fear

though it's just a trick of light
that turns a blowing branch
into a grasping arm,
just the shudder of wind, the panes empty.

Outside our window the river mirrors a white barn, floats
lights up and down its other side.
It sucks in grey sky some days,
leaves a blanket of fog to cover its deeds.

There are doors no one will open for us,
windows we are forced to look through,
out past our own reflections. Windows that look
into someone else's past. And in some lifetimes

we are always looking in. In some rooms
we always feel trapped. Nothing we do
is enough. No one we love
fills us. Like dark inside water,

some longing never leaves. We don't know the cure,
just the wind's cold shoulder. Nothing can shutter
the sadness of windows. Their long endurance.
All the light they let in.

The Fern Kidnappings

No one lives in Cape George lighthouse
        but a small, obedient box always on duty
        reading, beaming back to town
        what it reads: wind speed,
        absence of warmth (never a very
        sizzling plot). Another cold, little spring & whoever
        runs this show has distended daylight
        into a dimness that appeals
        to thieves.
                We cruise the cape,
        spade trunked in our white sedan
        borrowed from the bank. We have nothing
        of our own; this is why the woods
        owe us something; why we're out
        kidnapping ferns. We've been married
        long enough to see the pleasure
        in transgression; we've done our homework.
        The back roads have back roads, handwritten signs:
        Rear Settlement, Rear Georgeville.
        We've read some ferns
        are sexy, some aren't. We want
        the sexy ones: netted chain, hart's tongue,
        ostrich. We've reached a wet depression,
        a tall zoo of filmy plumes. You dig, I bag,
        & hurry, I say, before night
        falls. Surprising how much they don't want
        to come with us, these whiffs of green air, of lace
        tracking finely up the stem
        only to end as hostages, held
        by a couple of thugs from a subdivision
        who sit in the dark, watching dumb letters
        scroll across a screen:
                Conditions at Cape George . . . Conditions . . .

The Valley, After Blossoms

In Annapolis Royal, we stepped on a soldier
dead for two hundred years: sorry:
what else could we say? Then we had drinks.

A full professor I know doesn't want his wife
wearing dead people's clothes. This is based
on a false syllogism.

In the apple capital, Berwick
Frenchy's over the feed store, we fill our baskets
with glorious rags, new school clothes

silver dinner dress, anorak. What goes around.
These are stories of human exertion, sweat
stains under white t-shirt arms. Labour, a whole

wall of maternity clothes. Weighty ambition, epic
shoulder pads. Seduction, tiny crotchless things
in the far bin. Brooks Brothers suit (my husband

says in case there's a funeral). The place
smells like New England, old L.L. Bean. I wear
someone's Nantucket sundress, good for me. We are

what the ships drag in, what we unearth, warp
and woof, here's a dog sweater, they've thought of
everything (warm loyalist pets). A doll with

pathos for a face. A suit of armour in case
there's a war. The blossom festival was
last weekend; aside from that, things remain

quiet, the cashier says, sorting a tray of buttons.
Aside from the occasional squabble over high
end linen, the odd "this is to die for"
cried out in pure wool ecstasy, rebirth.

Muskoxen

Great, dark skirts moving across Bering bridge,
                                    flank to flank, centuries
ago,
what do we know?

They have one living relative in northern Tibet.
Their ruts have been mistaken for sea ice breaking.
There has been one albino sighting (1853).
They have built-in snow goggles.
They are the opposite of hummingbirds.
They turn, in flight, into a single, beating heart,
                        a swoosh of black kilt against sedge (still,
they can't cover
            all the angles).
They have their heroes.
They form a garland around their calves, under siege, an ebony
                                    crown of thorns.
Their helmeted horns double as vegetable diggers.
They are dressed for the apocalypse.

Brave

is a word you must grow
into, wait while it sheds
its patronizing skin. *Be brave*, taller people
said in waiting rooms.

Brave

needs to season like wine your mother made
from dandelions between chores meant for a man

twice her size. No wonder she made her own
yellow medicine, asterisks of summer to soothe backaches.

Not so dear as store-bought.

She is eighty-three now, shorter
than you. With her in the examining room
your skull fills with the lilacs
she heaped over your birthdays
to cover the absence of gifts.

The doctor says *curvature of the spine*.
From a life of farming, she says.

You want to say it's the way any mauve branch would
bend into May. You want to say it's only the dance of the brave,
tenacious spring. Bones at a glance, you want to say
tell so little. You've been watching her for years, only
now see her, a brave woman with lilacs
picking her way along the white, gnarled path,
the vertebrae of love.

What We Learned on the Highway Near St. John's

That bakeapples are not baked, or apples.
Two boys waving jars above their heads. In grand sweeping arcs.
   We thought "accident," but

why the jars? We pulled our rampant-with-rust American car over.
   No sign of blood.
No camero slicing the grizzled bush. The boys were freckled, as
   boys in summer
are. Denim torn at the knees.

   We opened our windows.

The jars were filled with floating, tiny, plush globes, the smallest of
    pumpkins.
Bakeapples, they said. *Best spooned over vanilla ice cream. Only grow
on the island*. They spoke of muskeg & thorns, hours of hunting.

We bought all four, pleased what we thought
an accident was a new way of knowing
apples. Driving away, we looked back at the boys,
                                    waving, their hands empty.

when night meets thread & needle & lies down among the bedclothes

This night begins in scraps — blue velvet
sky & water. Timeworn, but indispensable to eye,
to skin. As colours fade, my needle
cuts a path for figures, their movement lending
interest, shape. The birds by now are
knots to hold the trees in place. And that singing you hear

at the edges? My mother. Her sister, Kay.
On their way home from a dance. This thread comes
from a story someone told me. And from Moon, who poured a path-
way to the beach & set them
laughing, full skirts gathered up in fists & bare feet suction-
cupping cold wet sand. And reeled them

up the ladder, to the loft of this old fish shack . . . so
to sleep. These tassels you can roll between your fingers
are the *lap lap lap* of each small wave, as
clear, distinct, as certain as a sister's breath
beside her. Shots of silver for the gaps
along the beams. They are 19. They are 21

or 22. The nap, like seagrass, parts
to make their way.
Sleep now, child. Pull
this night around you. Even as the sky grows lights, starts bleeding
into vivid pink. To lavender. The start
of blue. Moon still out, a pale swatch. Their shoes

are swinging from their hands. Feet wet with dew. And this
is where my needle
pauses. A stitch
before this

shadow in the distance, on the
doorstep turns

to Papa,
Papa quaking:
the disgrace you have brought   on this house!
And Moon, the younger sister
who began the trouble, wills herself invisible
& fades away.

Lay the raw
silk of a dawn like this against your cheek.
Their legs are young & strong, arms resting
on each other's shoulders. The needle & the breath
held. The first birds about
to sing.

especially after rain, the gulls

Earth is a stadium
& the crowd is going wild tonight, the crowd

wants blood. Why
are they squawking so loudly

out there on the island? No more
fish guts on the breakwater, or tossed

off the side of a boat
for them? Or were they always like this, & I just

don't remember? It sounds like
something has to give, something has to happen.

The stadium roof will blow off tonight
or the gulls will pick the land-

scape up, yank it free
of the bedrock that holds it, pull away

what's green & fine,
roots dangling like the stuffing of Salvation

Army furniture.
Especially after rain, the gulls

are flapping (unhinging)
wings in unison, against

white bodies, preparing
to carry the island away

in their scavenger beaks & take it
. . . where?

This is the body, consoling itself

This is the body in solitude
making a companion of itself
& noticing how it makes a companion of itself —
how it's made up of so many pairs.
How right hand & left hand
                              clap
      in *time, time, time*
together, how they work up
a heat.
How fingers entwine
in a gesture of prayer,

a twiddle & whorling
of thumbs. Here's the body

pausing in the doorway, middle
of the afternoon, arms folded   neat
beneath the sullen weight
of breasts . . .

here comes the rolling:
*front*foot to   *front*foot
body entering the room.

At times like this the body
is so happy in itself
                    it seems to float
above the mattress, curled
on its side in the wash of light.
Licks of air sift
through the screen.
A wind chime in the distance
is a skeleton of small
bones dancing. Hand alights
on flutter-
pulse of throat.
Now, the knees
tuck further up, calves jostle into place
together. One arm bends
to cradle head sinks deeper
into pillow, eyes grow-
ing heavy&heavier
lids coming
down.

This is when the begging bowl of mind
tips over. And tongue, that old amphibian
in the upper reaches, is one of the last
to stop registering
                    things. Darting like a gecko
on the chamber ceiling, sliding

into molars, fat & brazen
as a bullfrog. The warmth of tongue being
its only concession
to human.
                    That, & how it searches
till it finds a loose tooth, jagged edge
or taste of blood just underneath
the surface
& goes back
& goes back there again.

the body as dictionary, as bible
(for m.)

i.

the framing and line of your neck
and collarbone, this morning, that has, in some

oversight or some mistake, been wrongly christened
by the anatomists; that has been called (in

the texts given to students of the body)
by something other than its true name: *home*.

ii.

it is taken on faith, really: i reach
for you, the cool fluorescence of the kitchen

at night a sort of fitting backdrop — setting off
your summer's tan. and my hands slowly along

your sides, then fingering the rosary of your surprise,
my touch, the effect of night and its airs.

snow; a fear of dying

The plan is the body.
The plan is the body.
The plan is the body.
        — from "The Plan Is the Body" by Robert Creeley

the plan is the body —
is in the physicality of all this as i glance out
the window. and there, the november light is
in its solid form — frozen, pieced and chopped —
falling from the trees like ticker-tape. announcing
victories and deaths, conclusions of all sorts. and
the wind outside is moderately strong: it can be
heard, and it can be seen in the nervous postures
of birch and spruce. and this snow, it is
a smart suggestion, really, of what

      the plan is. the body
knows that familiar swirling towards a destination, down.
and i am certain there was something like it swirling
in my mother's blood, in my grandfather's veins — something
snow-pale and rare, and not quite right; some thing
that seemed to come and go, but was truly weather constant.
and that blood certainty is mine — an arterial legacy, a
flowing probability of days, weeks and years. it is a cool
flow, this icy thickening that racks and scrapes and slows
me from the inside; it is hidden proof of

      the plan. is the body
that much a diagram, a window-framed picture, a
second-hand mapping or charting? on days like these
it would seem to be, so now i am obsessed with nature —
with its understated tallies: blood's snow and its piling
virus-frantic. i am concerned with ideas of pressures and
systems, with the way seasons bleed into each other
like colours, and the fact that drifts melt to newly grown
green; that even here we always return, however
briefly, to crumbling earth and fields, and stones.

a move to liquid

there's a ceremony for everything, some take so long years can pass
before you realize how much has changed; even you are no
longer yourself.
> — *from* "I Know Women" by Sue Goyette

there's a ceremony for everything
these days; i suppose there always has been — so
it should have come as no surprise that i sliced my hand
in the slick warmth of doing dishes one afternoon
in the days following your departure — a sort of ritual, a
bloodletting or a cleansing. it was under the strain of
the temperature's disparity; the cool shock of rinsing,
that the glass understood its hidden fissures all at once, and
cracked. and the fact that, in this instance, the breakage was
so quick, so immediate, is an intriguing one — given that

some take so long. years can pass
in the breaking in some cases — with favourite mugs or
cups falling gradually into disrepair, slowly chipping away,
until they are eventually diminished so much that they
hardly resemble their former selves. it was to be expected, this
move to liquid — to blood, to water — given all the indiscriminate
reaching we do, the fumbling about in the murky pools of
our days; given that the movement is at once both quotidian
and filled with an undeniable danger — a possibility of violence:
of a misplaced steak knife, a plate chipped some indeterminate
time

before. you realize how much has changed
only when, in reaching through the water, the former
crispness of it is missing. only when you notice, however slightly,
that some quality is gone, that the sink is no longer a stinging heat;
that it is instead a tepid jumble of unseen edges. and when this
fluid complacency takes hold, when it clings to and greases
your hands, your reaching — that is when the sudden ceremony
of shattered glass or some other domestic ritual is most

likely to occur. and really, considered for a moment, it does make
sense: that it would happen in this way, at this time when

  even you are no longer yourself —
distracted or distanced from your actions, from your interaction
with all else; a time when your own comprehension of
the most simple things is a cloudy swirling, a sullied mixture, a
greying mess. it is in this dulled uncertainty of down-time,
of your submersion in the everyday, that the sudden pain will
surface; will appear and announce itself in a sort of liquid
language — a baptismal wound that in its stinging flow serves
to remind you that there is still in you, at any given moment, a
keen ability to feel; the possibility of unexpected change.

a winter's affection; radiomimetic
  (for m.)

> *In recent years a number of chemical substances have been*
> *found which produce biological changes that are very similar*
> *to, often indistinguishable from, those produced by atomic*
> *radiations. . . . Other similarities were soon discovered*
> *between the biological effects of radiation and mustard gas*
> *and a related chemical substance known as nitrogen mustard.*
>   — from *Atomic Radiation and Life*
>   by Peter Alexander

  almost molecular: it is ridiculous, i know,
this attempt of mine at an adequate metaphor

for how profoundly you have touched me. but,
in fact, it would seem there is some scientific precedence

for this. this is history
repeating itself, but mutated. this is you, like nitrogen

mustard. and just as the muddy confusion
of europe, (its foggy gasping), smothered

not only men in their flailings, but eventually
the very anger in their blood, announcing

solution — so too you arrived in the unseasonable mild
and churning of a solitary eastern february

and precipitated change, discovery. and now,
months later, still at times i am choked,

my lungs stilted and heavy, with you, with this
exposure. and so this is me, affected; this is me

— the unlikely beneficiary of
your radiance, of you, like nitrogen

mustard, radiomimetic. ridiculous, i know, but true.

Heron

Neck tucked in
like a sackbut,
    legs trailing

looser than use,
it shoulders a
    collop

of sky. Inside
is the man who
    tried

to enter its skin.
His skull sharpened
    down

to a quill point,
reptilian, curt,
    amber-eyed.

Woodcock Feather

As light as whatever you wish,
some fostering fall, perfection
of snow or the tiptapping brush

of a leaf. November, and look
we're still here. I've thought
how we once broke cover, our quick

double flight shaped out
of moss and grass, leaving
this scapular feather. Soft, is it

slate? Is it ash? Grey, my love,
shading to rufous, a form
interfusing, allusive:

spreckled, barred, streaked, a gather
of mottle and margin, or touch, or
breath we also have drawn together.

Kestrel

So much for its stiff-quilled stoop,
its beak's obstetrical slash,
grandeurs, foiled, counterfeit voices,

the wince of surrogate violence
gripping a shape into earth.
Kestrel keeps clear, the name

and the cry it makes, *killy*,
buff, slate, hover of kingfisher
wingbeats converting to flight

away, fall, flared back and stalls
on a tree tip, wings
cockered shut that instant.

Escalade
(Paul-Émile Borduas, 1905-1960)

Tell him of apples, roads, friends
the kingfisher's clatter and clang
of a pillaging jay. Quote words

he once offered: *Wasn't I born
too soon, in an immature country?*
Use his stream's transformation

as trope, its planes skewed aslant, their
foldings, slidings wrinkled as wind
ruffles up and boats he'd rather

have built patter lightly as paint
drops: *Let suicide cease in
Canada to be the sole honest*

*solution to the tragedy
of our poets.* Schismatical
brother-in-arms, he could nearly

convince all but the absolute
mad, and his paintings condemn
the rest to castles in Egypt

return of the imprisoned sign,
flight of ephemeral dancing,
catacombed rock sunk in wine.

Crabapple Blossoms

1

Light, and light's duplicity,
        they flaw in a scud, haul
juddering back, snubbed,
        sway halt and sounds
of dark water, song sparrows
        lucent by water, shake
each loosening spray.

2

Conclusive of nothing, themselves
        most of all, their scent is
a trace of the rose
        become new, staying old, a play
of immaculate presence, stone
        being stone; wood, wood;
blossoms, blossom.

3

White, pink under white
        where the calyx held. Wind away now,
earth remains as promise. How
        much is enough? All there was:
blossom unfalling, its
        whiteness falling,
wherever you break to touch.

Deer on a Beach

Once in Africa I heard voices wailing, then turned a bend
in a muddy track and saw the wagon full of women,

faces greased with white, like a chorus from a Greek tragedy,
reminders — strophe and antistrophe — of what was lost.

Yesterday, when the beach was blindfolded with snow,
I found parts of a deer. My daughter wouldn't look

at the elegant hoof (which I lifted with the tip
of my boot) or the half-ellipse of jawbone. She hung back,

afraid, while I examined the hide, and the way it seemed
to be cut, slashed from the body. I could see the lining

of red, like an opera cloak. The head was gone, and the antlers,
but I didn't think about this until further up the beach,

where I saw the two forelegs, stuck in a drift
of snow feathered with animal hair. Grief has no words,

only a trailing off into things remembered
inaccurately. Months ago we'd seen a doe a half-mile away,

sleek and young, in the sparse woods above the beach, her flanks
heaving gently. We left the beach — where the ocean had thrust

glassy fragments of ice into the soft strip of land — and climbed
the steps to a little deck. Below us, the remnants of the deer

cast here and there, did not keep us from looking further out
to where the frozen sea, in folds and dips and pans, spread white,

unmoving. But something had changed, as if a lock in the cold air
had clicked open with a key. The ice was cracking, abruptly;

we shuffled up the next slippery flight of steps,
and through the woods. We saw crisscrossed tracks

of deer and dog, and perhaps snowshoe hare, though human
prints obscured them in places. I thought of the deer's small, cloven

hoof, and its fur, threaded brown and gold. Trophies not taken. Nothing
was left but tidbits for the crows: such food, stinking of violence,

comes from our world, not the next. Death gets into it
one way or another, a voice that follows wherever we go.

White, Mauve, Yellow

> "The bowl does not have colour in itself; light generates
> the colour."
>
> — Johannes Itten

A bedsheet is suspended on the clothesline
in my neighbour's yard. I am surprised by the
rippling white as the sheet lifts
and exposes the greenish-brown grass below.
This square — although slightly more than a square,
less than a rectangle, opening out in the wind
like a body waiting for another body,
a loosening, stretching
length of singing white on that single
float of wind, appearing whiter because of the mauve
shadow underneath — changes immediately

when the wind slackens. Hanging
like a stranded piece of wing, it is the colour of
something caught, animal or bird
or even the skin at the wrist and the slightly creamy
white of the inner arm, paler than any other part
of the body and more secretive. The sheet snaps briefly,
flips over the clothesline and slaps the air again.

Now it is still, a painful white,
an almost perfect shape,
except for the curling hem and the undulating
pink stripes along the top and bottom. The shadow
on the grass should be taken into account too,

because of its darkness
in contrast, and its shape, which is long
and distinct as a memory, except for one
scrolled edge. My neighbour appears, pulling the line
which makes a sound like a cat crying
as she takes the five pegs out of the sheet,
bundling it in her arms, so that it seems
yellow, heaped up like that, and I imagine her
putting it on a queen-sized bed,
briskly tucking it in, so that it is entirely
flat and smooth.

A Name, Many Names

I knew you
long before I saw you:
one thing inside another,
making itself up. Lightly
snow fell, kept falling
the night you were born —

like those prayers tied
to branches by the Japanese —
scissored bits of paper,
each one a word,
a name, many names, loose
in the dark.

You'll need a name
that's door and window, roof
and bed. You'll need a name to trick
the thief that comes
to live in your heart. But now
you need a name so diaphanous
and small
it takes its shape from air.

The Lilacs

This is not tenderness: the lilacs hanging in the rain,
     my breath
coming in gasps, the dog shaking herself beside me.
     I'm thinking of the slap

in the day when the light goes. The puncture, the sigh
     of something pricked
by a blue that has no edge. Your lungs, collapsed
     bubbles, whatever

draws air, keeps us going. She found the keys, drove you
     to Emergency
in her stocking feet. Into that rising panic —
     a snap: any flower

broken from its branch. Along with this: the mauve,
     dark purple, wealth
of the new. Rain, fathering the blooms. Here,
     everything

I've been so slow to offer up. All those hours
     spent reading
the mirror. A little cloud, exhaled, distorts every
     reflection. We're not kings,

or fools, or third daughters. We're only the makings
     of ourselves. You,
with a cord trailing on the carpet, one end for the oxygen,
     one for the body,

like the snake's tail, the swallowed circle, that keeps
     this hour, this rain,
each tiny opened bud alive. Yanking the leash,
     the dog pulls me on

to something else, her nose deep in the beaded grass.
     Then down the hill
on Brookland and round the bend, my hand burning
     wet from the lilac's candle.

Bare Places

There are bare places
inside us
like the ground under children's swings,
the corners of old pastures
where only bones grow,
hideouts
smaller than pores
in which the acceptable
festers, golden resorts
where we bury
our heads in white sand,
convinced we are
alone.
But we never travel
alone. The anonymous
insider
arrives at the terminal
just ahead of us
knowing there are no planes
on the runways, nothing
but the slow cattle of the moon,
their udders glowing,
swinging heavily
with the knowledge of strange grass.

Skull

Winter makes a last stand
in stippled ditch-ice
　　　our black boots slide over
like otters.
　　　　　We hear

mad trappers
screaming through the fissures,
　　　　　　　　　　　the fractures; Napoleon
in a syphilitic rage
　　　　　　　staggering out of Russia . . .

Knife-wind from the north. Empty skates
lie at the mouth of a culvert.
　　　　　We turn west and head across the wet
fields, mica-layered ice, brown grass, a lip
　　　　　turns blue
just above the horizon. I look down. Where
　　　　have I seen this animal's discontented skull before?

Walk After Rain

Near evening, the first days
of December,
we walk the fields,
the cattle trails.
Apples all over
Nova Scotia, innocent
and heavy, have turned
to mud. Up the ridge, smoke
drifts down from O'Brien's

like a lost scarf floating home.
Hoofprints
beside a low drinking place,
the run-off trickling
miles through spruce to the strait and winds
pushing, pushing.
Two deer,
        moth-coloured, stare
from the edge of the alders.
They are the first to turn
and go.
        Magi-blue
        sky, new stars.
Mist, the sad guest,
        waiting by the barn.

Multiple Choice

"Fragrant" or "fragment," I still can't decide which
It was then spiralling out of her mouth, eager, touching
Down on the back of the hand I was going to brush her
Cheek romantically with, but drew back at the last
Instant (even more romantically), pinned between the two
Words I heard but didn't hear (there was only
One, of course, and it might have led to love,
Sex, trips to the dentist with kids), but because
I couldn't be sure, because I couldn't own the one word
That wasn't, and because she refused to seem the type
To repeat herself with lips hovering over the soft froth
Of café au lait, I let it all go: the lips,
The sex, the intertwined urban-vegetable-market-espresso bar
Afternoons, all for the *false compare*, the single's single
Look back along the tracks, wondering how, how it would have
Ever gotten beyond the first fever, the fierce fumbling,

The decades of discontented familiarity, the stumbling forward
Together and finally tumbling into the ravine hunched up
Holding hands and performing unrehearsed together
A perfectly harmonious grovelling throat-rattle.

from **The Killed**

Returning, near morning,
a boy, about sixteen, sitting in the back
of a dirty, three-wheeled truck, shovels and spades
pick-up sticks around him on the ground,
smell of diesel soaking the air.
Both doors open, no driver,
just the boy sitting there, staring,
as we walked toward him.
The crater must have been three metres,
a deep shadow under the truck.
The boy looked untouched, just dry clay
on his boots, smudges on the back of his hands,
a smear on his cheek. Someone thought he was from _____,
about six kilometres away. Then we saw
why the stare was so remote.
The side of the truck
was soldered to him, fused
to his back like scorched armour,
ending at the shoulders. The back of his head
was gone, hair, skin and
blood scabbed across the window of the truck cab.
We had to move.
We knew troops would be coming for him.
But which side?
We left the road and kept walking, a few metres
within the trees. There were bees, working early.
Wind like a truce through the metallic sheen of leaves.

Haunting

A house I once lived in now calls out to me,
strange cats leaning off its porch roof like gargoyles
batting lazily at evil spirits and June bugs.
You see, the house is unhappy with its present tenants.
Their drapes misunderstand the windows,
their furnishings misuse the unusual layout of the kitchen.
I doubt they've ever sat and listened to the strange music
of the house at midnight, one board grinding against another,
strummed by some local wind, exiles singing their former lives.
I suspect they've never noticed the peculiar lollop of the
    floorboards
or that the taps turn different ways at every faucet,
that there are light switches that operate nothing.
They've covered the walls with large pastel posters of flowers,
filled the rooms with their inhospitable possessions.
I've seen them through their evening window,
reclining vacantly before the TV.

It drives me crazy, the house's call.
It aches in my bones,
a dampness haunting a meadow.
They don't know I'm watching.
Even their cats look through me.
It's as if I'd never lived in my own house.

Is this what it's like to have once loved a stranger's wife
and to bump into them now on the street?
Seeing her with him, inappropriate him,
are you angered at his indifference towards you?
When he looks away as she talks with you,
taps a cigarette out of the packet without offering one
to either of you, do you think *I could still map*
the delicate regions of her body from memory,
but he knows nothing of this woman. Nothing!

wishing to drop some hint, some detail
to spook him just a little?

Some night, drunk or exhausted, I'll stumble up that driveway,
cats watching me from the edge of the roof.
And while the unimaginative tenants sleep
I'll walk into that now strange kitchen,
the door opening easily to me,
and move things noisily around.

Winter Marsh

We have wintered in the poems of John Thompson,
grown lean through January February March
et cetera while frost overran everything,
like Jerusalem artichokes.

Yet there are mild days when a walk on the marsh is tolerable,
road intermittently windswept bare and drifted deep,
with a sombre dog as escort.

Here, eye follows the abandoned rail line
counting distances in hydro poles,
dog flushes a chorus of tiny birds
from a wiry thicket,

everything's a breath of the palest blue,
the hollow instant before any action.

Always something lurks.
Do you think of death out here?
Just roads. Just skies.
And Colville's black winged bird.

Undergoing
Jewish General Hospital, Montreal
6:35 a.m.

Keeping vigil for minimum wage,
"a non-trained attendant,"
I watch
the red sawn bone
of the amputee,
blaspheme by writing this
while his moans go on
as if pain could be reduced
to an even rhythm, suspiration,
be neutralized.
But the pain goes on
between the next cigarette,
another pill.
He has a cross of scars
on his chest, has suffered
seven, "*sept opérations.*"
The stump,
the red sawn bone
of this grizzled undergoing
man.
There is no pain like this pain.
This is not God's.
This belongs to the son of man.

On the Beach One Day

The girl was swimming nude
when the car drove up, bumping
among the dunes; and inside it
they spotted her bathing suit
wrinkled on the sand.
One of them retrieved it, hung it like a
pennant on the aerial and
the car spun off in the sand soft
like talc.
                When she saw this happening
she ran from the waves, cried
at them, the roar of the car
came over the roar of the ocean
on that long white deserted beach.
Then they circled and came back,
hooting at her, honking their horn,
to sweep around her, then drove off —
panties flickered in the wind —
she followed, one hand between
her thighs, the other on her breasts,
running after the receding car;
the men laughed back at her,
hooted some more. She
couldn't catch up; exhausted, she
sank to her knees in the sand,
a signal. They veered back,
steering in a tightening, widening circle,
closing in, retreating, "ye-aaaah,
ye-aaaah," they screeched at her.
The sun stood high, the waves
bubbled on the sand, she let
that sand cover her, another suit.
Through the tall afternoon, the car blared,
the men yelped, through the wide white
afternoon the sea came toppling
                on her body.

Auden's Face

Much of any poetry's dispensible, but
observe his face. A runic face, cracked
like baked clay, mud-veins left
by the drying sun. What are these hieroglyphics,
this dry irony of skin? Read the message
of the temple broken open, the ark
desecrated. Was there ever a time better
than the one in which he lived? The sun
told him no. Bleached bones in a salt land
said don't forget us. Age limned
the parchment with memory, decay; life scored
the tablet vertical, horizontal. Writing words
carefully looked up, he sought precise truth, kept
life in one pocket, work in another —
like pencils. This was Auden's face. He
chose, was given these serious ruins,
the mark of bitter weather.

Father on My Shoulders

> *Haste, my dear father . . .*
> *And load my shoulders with a willing freight*
> — The Aeneid
> *translated by John Dryden*

Everyone looked away
passed without speaking
by their silence they mocked me
for believing in him at all —
Pay no attention to their looks,
I reassured him.

He seemed to tire more quickly than usual.
I feared the journeys
were becoming too much for him
I hoisted him up.

(He was so like a bird now
bone, skin, even the hard forearms
  withered
I could carry him with ease.)

We walked along the beach
beside the mountains he had crossed.
Fishermen were throwing square nets upon the water.
There were so many tiny fishes in the sea
they could hardly haul in their catch.
This would interest him. But no.

He said nothing.
For the first time
his weight seemed burdensome.
Finally he spoke:

This is no good,
for a young man
to be seen carrying around
his dead father.

Then he asked to be let down.
He went on his way with light step
in the direction from which he had come
freed of the terrible needs of the living.
I saw him no more.

Revelations

For God's sake
come up out of the cellar —
the world I tell you
is not going to end in the morning.

Neither with thunder nor fire —
that's the vision of boy children
their pale necks chafed red
by their starched collars.

This is how the world ends
if you want to know:
I go out one morning
to feed my bullcalf.

And as I always do
I get down on my hunkers
to watch and listen
to him feed awhile.

His snout flecked
with the grain
he looks up, sees me
slumped down — asleep.

And in the whole great sounding box
of the barn, there is only
the music of his soft face
in the trough.

River Otters at Play

Love
as it ought to be made:
leisurely, buoyant, liquid.
The river otters roll
over, the male a hapless sailor
holding hard to the capsizing
keel of the female.
Over
        and under
they sink,
bubbling desire, emerge
        au pair
sucking night air,
circling together,
        clasped
one to the other —
otter to otter.

Love as play,
in this they are always
faithful and true.
Love made as such things

ought to be done, with grace,
                for fun.
I have seen them before,
not locked like this,
but moving free,
                in synchrony
dive and surface together,
anxious to spy the other's face —
okay, they say, and dive again
weaving their submarine passions.
Or on the slippery bank,
                slide
over the other's oily back,
musking each other
as they enter water,
each quick, sleek movement
a kind of foreplay,
sensing the other's wet wishes.
Now they are in no hurry;
as the light fails
they court the dark waters,
stirring them,
and, deep down,
limbic me.

Dragging Bottom

A chain mail hand, a titanic dustpan
stirs a turmoil of sediment in its wake,
furrows the sea floor. A ploughshare
that keeps on going beyond land's end
over endless wet horizons, leaving
the sea bottom cross-hatched as a griststone.
A horn blows, the capstan sings, a maul is swung,

the drag belches the benthos onto the deck.
Life so lowly, it most resembles globs of oil
but for the holes at either end, mouth or anus
(who knows?) that filters water endlessly as thoughts.
Eels excitable as neon, animals turned inside out,
with skin rough as stucco.
And this magnificent fish, big and flat as a coffee table,
wide wings spread for undersea flight — landed here.
A man, sore and numbed, hefts the biggest stone he can
to crush the skull of this monarch of the deep,
then kicks the brained fish through the scuppers
to sink. This is our shame, repeated again and again.
What we cannot sell, we kill or leave to die.
It is only these, a treasure chest
of calcium dollars, we stoop to gather.
Curved knives flash between hard halves, lift,
the top springing open like a locket
to reveal a cameo of viscera.
A flick of the wrist feeds the ever-vigilant hags
that plane and parry, shearing water.
The horn blows, men take cover, the deck
raises like a drawbridge, dumps everything,
half-alive or dead, back into the sea.
This is our shame, repeated again and again,
until there is nothing but stones and broken shells to spend.

The Text of Evening

Suppose, for instance,
in that one spangled pause
of day's final sentence — lilacs
persistent as the must of old books —
a trout should flash above water
and hang an instant in the dusk
like some unsponsored meaning
teased from black pools of print.

Sentiments rich in uncertainty,
in promise,
may swoop like nighthawks
through the numinous air,
or cut across time's clear current
like the voices of children
belling over the damp grass
and under the looming trees.

Even so, even
if the twitterings of roosting birds
should come out of those trees
almost intelligible, almost
like the voice of Hermes,
what will they mean after all,
what alter or fulfill?

Trout back on the underside
of evening, small bells
stilled into silence, into sleep,
and birds settled mute in the leaves,
lights along the country road will open
one by one — flickering moments
held stolidly in place
like words in line on a page.

Homesteading

Once, driving the dirt road
that cut straight across the Rawdon hills,
the grade ahead a red slash rising steep
through the afternoon, we stopped
at an old place off to the left.
Maybe this time it would be the right one,
the one he was always looking for
in the newspaper or out along those country
roads — whose ruin he could rectify.
Whose price he could afford.

It was late, just befor dusk.
Like a family, three generations of us
gone from home, we bounced up the lane
to the yard where chickens once pecked,
dieselled to a stop by the greyboard house.
There were sheds, a sagging barn,
stony pastures skirted by acres
of blowdown and raspberry tangle.

"Ain't she a humdinger?" Granddad said,
no more than a sliver of irony in his tone.
Fireflies pulsed in the long grass
around the place as he pointed out
this and that to Nan and Mom, how short
a walk it was to the well, the file
of alders below the house that told us
there was water on the property,
or how he might put running water
in the kitchen. At the very least.

My sisters fussed in the back seat
of that old Ford coupe of his he'd bought
cheap, thoroughly used since '48.
They were cranky, worn out from hanging
onto the hand straps down every back road

in Hants County, through every clutch
of houses with a name — Ardoise, Stanley,
Shubenacadie — learning no more than the landscape
of failure, abandoned farms leaning into hillsides
or settling to earth in a grove of dead elms.

Nothing better to do, I wandered
down to the water, followed its windings
into the trees, picking up stones
from the current to hold the comfort
of smooth edges in my palms, taken in by flashes
of fish, leaves jittery with wind,
what was left of the light.

And then I saw it, a long-legged stillness
in the moving water, neck like a crooked stick,
hunger gleaming in its jewelled eye.
A band of last light flinty on the blackness
spread flat between us, I stood there
watching, wanting only this vigil
above fish or whatever its head
darted down to, once, and once again,
this creature that knew what it was looking for
and where to go to find it.

Green Cadillac

Mornings we hold on for noon,
for sandwiches, cold drinks,
moments to take a look
at the landscape, or water
glinting in the distance,
remote as the feeling
of someone else's dream.

The afternoons have waited
for us all our lives:
a young woman, alone,
passing in a green Cadillac
along this slash of asphalt
dividing woods and blue water;
the horny talk of bored
and lonely men — who all need
the work. But if it rained
no one would care.

There are days when it won't
end, the body pulling
from daylight into dusk
through the dissonance of machines
and the sun's glare on hot tar,
acrid hours shimmering in the distance,
strung out ahead
flat as rolled pavement.

Resurrection at West Lake

Ringed by dark palisades
of spruce and this cold, black
bowl of water, I understand again
about words, how folded wings

can open, lift into flight:
love, when it batters us,
or *death*, when we sense its swoop,
a wendigo stirring in shadows.

This one-crow sky leans on my bowels.
My eyes are admonished

by witch fingers of naked poplars
forming their mute adjurations.

And social voices fall silent too:
crows, chickadees, whisky-jacks
contain their clatter; squirrels
grow mute as pine cones.

Up on the ridge behind me
thin, bone-white remnants
of the deepest snowdrifts glow,
skeletal under the hackmatacks.

Out of these enigmatic evergreens,
around imponderable granite mounds,
beneath one flapping black rag
of crow, time's surge begins again.

PRINCE EDWARD ISLAND

Charlottetown Harbour

An old docker with gutted cheeks,
time arrested in the used-up-knuckled hands
crossed on his lap, sits
in a spell of the glinting water.

He dreams of times in the cider sunlight
when masts stood up like stubble;
but now a gull cries, lights,
flounces its wings ornately, folds them,
and the waves slop among the weed-grown piles.

The Island

Since I'm Island-born home's as precise
as if a mumbly old carpenter,
shoulder-straps crossed wrong,
laid it out,
refigured to the last three-eighths of shingle.

Nowhere that plough-cut worms
heal themselves in red loam;
spruces squat, skirts in sand;
or the stones of a river rattle its dark
tunnel under the elms,
is there a spot not measured by hands;
no direction I couldn't walk
to the wave-lined edge of home.

In the fanged jaws of the Gulf,
a red tongue.
Indians say a musical God
took up His brush and painted it;
named it, in His own language,
"The Island."

I've Tasted My Blood

If this brain's over-tempered
consider that the fire was want
and the hammers were fists.
I've tasted my blood too much
to love what I was born to.

But my mother's look
was a field of brown oats, soft-bearded;
her voice rain and air rich with lilacs:
and I loved her too much to like
how she dragged her days like a sled over gravel.

Playmates? I remember where their skulls roll!
One died hungry, gnawing grey porch planks;
one fell, and landed so hard he splashed;
and many and many
come up atom by atom
in the worm casts of Europe.

My deep prayer a curse.
My deep prayer the promise that this won't be.
My deep prayer my cunning,
my love, my anger,
and often even my forgiveness

that this won't be and be.
I've tasted my blood too much
to abide what I was born to.

The Squall

When the squall comes running down the bay,
Its waves like hounds on slanting leashes of rain
Bugling their way . . . and you're in it;
If you want more experience at this game
Pull well and slant well. Your aim
Is another helping of life. You've got to win it.

When you're caught in an eight-foot boat — seaworthy though —
You've got to turn your back, for a man rows backwards
Taking direction from the sting of rain and spray.
How odd, when you think of it, that a man rows backwards!

How odd, when you think of it, that a man rows backwards.
What experience, deduction and sophistication
There had to be before men dared row backwards
Taking direction from where they'd been
With only quick-snatched glances at where they're going.

Each strongbacked wave bucks under you, alive
Young-muscled, wanting to toss you in orbit
While whitecaps snap like violin strings
As if to end this scene with a sudden exit.

Fearfulness is danger. So's fearlessness.
You've got to get that mood which balances you
As if you were a bird in the builder's hand;
For the boat was built in consideration
Not only of storms . . . of gales too.

Though you might cut the waves with your prow
It'll do no good if you head straight to sea.
You've got to make a nice calculation
Of where you're going, where you want to be,
What you need, and possibility;
Remembering how you've survived many things
To get into the habit of living.

That Corrugated Look To Water

That corrugated look to water
— grey with a glitter:
I've been told now that it's ice;
microscopic bergs clashing,
making music of many thin tones
too faint for us to hear.

Gulls fly labouring
low and straight, point to point;
bouncing off air pressed down
by their own wingbeats,
tips walking on
the same wing tips reflected.

No day this for men
to be at business on the water
— no longer ours, but winter's.
Wind's so raw you don't know if
you're freezing or boiling;

though there are no waves, only
winking, glittering
ripples flittering against
downthrusting cold chunks

of air. We glimpse
it from the land through chinks
between hills, trees, houses;
and eyes ache
with brief sightings of
light shooting
flying needle
— icicle rays.

The Completion of the Fiddle
   (N.M.)

The fiddle's incomplete without the dance;
My darling. Let's hook fingers to complete
By motion to the calls, the sweet riddle
Of the tune now wriggling in the soft wind
On top of which the bright moon goes riding;
For if no happy bottoms prance and spin
Upon the planks and polish what's it all worth —
That round of steamed, shaped, rehardened wood
Varnished as it's put about a hollow
From which a tune may radiate its mirth
By the merry rub of gut against gut?
The candles flicker and the stars twinkle
All to be parts of the completed fiddle!

Out of the Blizzard

My sister and I've come out of the blizzard
for a wedding dress. Shaking off snow, she
says there are flowers I hardly know, how
impressive & expensive they are & which ones
not to carry. Certain kinds redden hands.
I'm maid of honour, shocking since she
was the bitch who said my friends secretly
hated me in grade eight & before that
fed me cold spaghetti from a garbage can
on our street. I'm learning to trust again
as she turns the cathedral gown into a person
I hated then needed as she snuck dark French
chocolate & love stories into the hospital
when I was allowed no visitors, especially
family. How hot that summer was, her tanned
legs crossed & uncrossed & rounded as she
ate for me. Hand-sewn sequins & pearls, the
saleslady coos — a summer wedding on the lake
after squalls.

The Boy I Never Met

In the docile light of Pinehurst
Park Terrace you become
the boy I never met. Whiter than
I imagined, the halls
a blizzard no one outruns.
You lean over your mother's chair

locking the wheels safe
while we say goodbye. This time
she cries. Her voice suddenly
lucid as anyone's
mother and how can you
leave her? Her sadness uncurls

pastel vines papering
the walls, sofa, there are
vines everywhere and along these
the urine creeps up. Over there
Frank is screaming
get him out of here

and women propped up in the hall look
like he speaks for them.
Her eyes river the powder
put on too thick and
her hand smears the pink she drew
into a smile for you, her son

from Canada. The nurses know
all about you and when we arrive
they're relieved. For one week
they won't hear how far away
you live. They can help her
to the bathroom,

change the bed,
hang up her clothes
and all they'll hear is
about real hamburgers, Woodland Park
and shopping every day.
Life made simple again

until the electric front doors
close like a gate
behind us. She will
stop crying, I say, taking your hand

as if you're the teenager driving
your mother back to Sedro Wooley when

things weren't as doctors thought. She
will wheel around to the patio
for a cigarette with Betty,
have dinner then bingo
and then sleep. I promise
she will sleep.

She Sends Him a Postcard of the Sea

Dear you,

the letter I haven't written explains
blue delphiniums
page six

Poppies didn't return so
weren't sent along with
the reasons for summer

Humid & tired bouts recurred
this week — beaches
crowded umbrellas & blond
children as I walked

the sand from Dalvay to
Tracadie dragging your name
like a stick

Teaching My Husband to Swim

Wind gathers the lake
like a rug then shakes it
up to his neck. Water
rises and I reassure
it's not deep
and he can't drown.
He coughs
as a speedboat shoots

waves dangerously
near his head.
It's okay
I say again swimming out
for the middle, a mistake
I realize too late.
Grown up in this body
of water, I've left

him too deep
into the past
where his mother stands
on a bridge
holding him
over the railing
ready to drop.
Two years old he

must look at the water
and kick, you'd wonder,
what the hell
was she thinking?
Cars slow. Someone
gets out. Stop her,
he is saying by the time
I swim to him.

DAVID HELWIG

Departures

It was the saints drove him out —
his wife's cold thighs, white lips,
the averted eyes, those were enough
to send a man to drink and hours
of solitude in his boat; still, at last,
it was the saints drove him out,
the fish-green, frog-yellow print
of St. Therese, the sacred hearts, the Jesuses
the wedding of that girl and the fool Joseph.

The wind sings against the cedar
shingles of the boathouse where he sleeps
with his gun and the fire of rum.
Slaughtered ducks lie in the slop
of the boat bottom like a mess of martyrs,
stinking of wet feathers and stale blood.

He hunts the mud inlets among the soft
voices of the reeds. In these hidden places
he is quick and sly as a mink, an excellent
killer of birds. Weather
is his first language now.
To live on water is to live
intimately with the sky. The intolerable
paper saints are gone. The voices
of the river are truer than any prayers.

Does she warm for the priest? he says
to the waves, to the November wind.
Does the name of Jesus bring the blood
to her face? The boathouse roof
too low to stand, he scuttles, bent,
to feed wood to the stove.

He is warm and fetid in his den.
He has gone to earth on an island
that floats between histories. Kills for the market
and smuggles hooch to the Yankee shore.
He plans a fusillade of holy gunfire
with saints and angels falling out of the sky like shot snipe.

In dreams his body is furred,
even his feet covered with tawny hair
to dance against the white belly, the white
breasts of the Little Flower,
virgin St. Therese. In dreams
he is animal and cruel and free.

He will die in midwinter and be laid out
among the holy pictures of the enemy.
It will take four strong horses
to drag his coffin away over the drifts.

from **On the Island**

1

A sudden risk of birds
slanting fast across
the night gloaming.

A single line of field
under a single moon.
The hare goes softly.

Light abandons the speaking
river. Still woods threaten
the possible, the haunted.

2

Simple as hymns these black sheep.
They have come across the long field
to illustrate their duty of presence,
called to be as all things in the day.

If the small hand does not
place the animals just so,
if each is not, intently,
the tangle of its shapes,
a day might go lame.

So to wake me travelling
these black sheep simple as hymns
have crossed the long field and wait
and patiently crop the spring grass.

Cape Breton in Autumn

We exist by what is half true
and our astonishment. The gulf
is a long vanishing from cliff
to thin horizon. Cranberries
grow two inches from the ground; whales
breach in the calm water near the shore.

Children at the edge of the land
watch the black fins rise and vanish,
as one after another the whales
breathe the white air and then go down
where vast unlikelihoods gather,
old Walt Whitman babbling a poem

in waves of white milk, little ones
adoring his bearded body.

But the lesson of cranberries
is only and always silence,
they are dark as dried blood, red tears,
small and perfect as haiku are,
and men stand in the ditch to pick
the wild fruit from the tangled growth
under a grey October sky,
the last harvest before freeze-up.

We live by our astonishment.
Between the eyes and the unseen
unknown beyond the horizon's edge
is all of poetry and what
we can choose to say. What we have
is immanent and almost true.

My Class Draws a Blank on Robbie Burns

If we forget where we come from
we move half blind through what we are.
I ask my mother and uncle, born Alexanders:
What part of Scotland, what clan?
Uncle Curt laughs, "We're Americans."
Not that I want a tartan, or my ancestors'
motto, other than that first I learned,
gimme liberty or gimme death. And Levi's
are my heritage, Disney's Crockett, John Wayne,
but blue jeans came from sail cloth, Genoese,
a Swiss merchant who saw the need
and that new clan of levellers who'd wear
one colour from Tennessee to Oregon.
And here, among descendants of the Highland
Clearances, the Famine, the Expulsion,
the name on lips is Calvin
Klein, and who the hell's Robbie Burns.
I'm glad you're now able to marry
across those old religious lines,
and that your grandfather's ghost won't grip
and guide your hand in the voting booth.
There's too much that needs loving
to wear old hatreds like a gunman's mask.
Roy plugs his fiddle into Peavey amps
and the old lament escapes
Cromwell's sword, while the step dancers'
heads bow down. When I ask my class
the difference between the two world wars:
one was black-and-white, one was in colour.
Yet that's more history than my potato-eating
forebears knew, travelling only as far as
their church to hear how God sent boatloads
of food to London as a test for His chosen.
We can have pizza or eggrolls day and night

and this is our glorious amnesia, entertained by
miniseries fragments of India and Rome.
The Shogun, Eva Perón and Old Possum
dance with Anne Boleyn and out
to the Green Gables store for ice cream
for old Hugh MacAuley's wake. At my grave
I want one of you who can still play the pipes.

Metamorphosis

In their bridal-white feathers the egrets
glide down to this Cuban beach,
their stately pose,
then lurch along the sand like Judy
McElroy in her elementary ballet
of polio braces across the minefield
at school, each step could detonate
ridicule, four-legged, cripple,
duck-walking, spastic. She was truly
what they call in warfare a hero
straight through enemy fire, without cover,
backup, or flinching, that same grim smile
that said (if it had been me), please
God, just let me reach the classroom
one more time without cracking, and falling
through those cracks to a dungeon where
I weep endlessly, rats begin to eat me alive, I am almost
a casualty, saved by the king's good
son, and they all
take my place in the rats' gnawing.

One morning we hide, snipers
behind a portable. Mick has brought
grenades, their thin

white shells, yolks
of flightless birds.
This is not me, but my hands
reach out, must have what Mick
passes around for protection
against the taunts that refusal would bring,
would contaminate me with Judy.
You can hear her coming, Meccano woman
clicking, scuffling. You can see us
leap out, shrieking baboons,
two or three of us hanging back, missiles
dropped or thrown wide of the mark,
but Judy is too cauled in egg white
and misery, twisting like a broken
windmill with her canes,
too robbed of whatever
kept her going, to notice any faces
peeled back to shame.
Why is it we rarely remember
what happens next? How Judy
made her exit, what cartoons
our separate minds played
at our first period desks.
Or if she watched from the classroom
windows our lunch-hour craving
to lunge and leap at baseballs,
each other. And with what
in her eyes. The tourists get too close
with their cameras, and the egret
extends its neck, unfolds its wings,
lifts away from our focusing.

Spark
(for Anna Percival, September-November 1993)

Little firefly
we would keep you
a little longer
at least one summer
in the evening yard
grass and branches
lit with your brief fire
the night field beyond our house
and around the veranda
we would keep you
our spark in the darkness
but you were called
by a voice full of flame
to help keep the great lights
burning, in a sky
full of fireflies
so distant, so near

Perfect Circle
(for Gerald and Shannon)

The crash in the living room is not
your son, his spaceship circles
a hostile planet upstairs, not his baby
sister with the ten keys of her
hands on your face, unlocked
and floating, a full
moon above her near-sleep.

The crash is the sound you see
as her face twists

the lid off a jar of cries,
your son veers into alien gravity
while you rush by, hammering the steps
down fast but nowhere near the speed of
the hawk that just crashed

through your window. A perfect circle
of languid grainy August air
in the glass, double-pane thick
a gale off the North Atlantic can't crack.
The red-tailed hawk on the smooth
branches of the white pine floor
shakes and shuffles its feathers

like a ballplayer knocked down by a
brush-back pitch, dusting himself off.
Once, flamboyant on the dance floor,
I slipped and flew and landed
on my tailbone: that perfect circle of
silence through which laughter poured.
You don't laugh. An arrow of the sky's

voracity has shot your house in the heart.
The method of release — hawk jumping
on the diaper-changing table,
bath basin dropped over it,
table wheeled outside —
is acceptable to the outstretched arm
that welcomed it back, message delivered.

The Digging of Deep Wells

involves
the breaking of solid ground,
stacking a circle's worth of sod
between tree stumps,
shovelling layers
of damp and musty clay
into wooden pails,
and soon requires
a ladder, and a tripod
of white-barked birch,
and where it's joined
a wooden block
through which passes
a hundred feet
of sturdy rope.
Then begins
the lining of walls
— fresh-cut sandstone
starts ten feet down,
builds up layer by layer
tight to the top.
Since there's no sign yet
of gurgling water,
the digger digs anew
goes down inside
the present ring of rock
with short-armed spade,
sharp and heavy crow,
hammers stubborn aggregate
smashes layered shale,
load after deadly load
sways up behind the rope.
The lower he goes,
the harder falling pebbles hit,

the deeper the darkness.
At ladder's full length
more layered circles of stone,
hole gradually widening
until this present wall
provides foundation
for the wall above
and by lantern light
the digger stands
on broken rock,
watches the ladder rise
and disappear above the rim.
The air is chill:
each clatter of crow
each scrape of shovel
each claustrophobic breath
echoes up the hole
toward the light
past the rain of dust
that coats the chilling sweat
of neck and brow.
And now at end of work
the bucket ends its day,
is swift unbound,
replaced by bosun's chair,
twirling he rises, to sleep
and then descend again
and again
until one afternoon
he stands in icy damp
hears the gush of stream
and fresh cold water rise up,
shock his weary groin.
Filled up with sudden joy
he risks to look
at what's above
and finds as his reward
a perfect circus of stars

Shingle Flies

In the spring
as sun warms
south faced shingles,
fat flies seduced
from winter slumber
drum dance
against my house.
I close my eyes,
travel backwards and look
through crack-paned windows
to a cold, musty room
walled with worn layered paper
wood floors rough and dusty
bare brick of chimney
standing watch near the door.
In that shabby space
at bright of morning
Billy draws his fingers
across my naked back.
I get three guesses
houses, cows, trees?
barns, pigs, tractors?
and then I draw on his
and he guesses
while the birds sing
and the flies buzz
drunk with sunshine
stupid with happiness

Me as an Archaeologist

I dig into your city; piece together your shattered pottery of desire.
I find bone fragments & tea leaves.
Bronze arrowheads of lust. Petrified, unleavened love.
Your fossil eyes gleam with salt.

In a dusty corner, I find flax seeds; plant flax.
Watch it sprout green as your youth, blossom
blue as your hot Mediterranean sea;
turn it into crisp linen.

I turn back crisp linen & sleep every night
between cool dreams of olives embroidered with spun gold.

Ancient gods sing. Their voices are streams of white
galaxies.
Below us the earth sings in a voice of dark loam & granite.

The moon, a rough & worn coin, wishes us luck in our madness,
our night of being wolves in the grey mountains.

I brush dirt, chip sediment from the hearth where you kept time,
where time hung in beaten copper kettles
full of lentils, barley & bay leaf, maybe parsley.

Your larder is full of old rice & desiccated pine nuts.

I dig into the rubble of your city & find
all these things preserved.
I know where your house is; I touch the old stone walls.

I want to hang a beaten copper kettle over your hearth,
fill it with brown rice, pine nuts,
strips of spring lamb. Season it all with cinnamon.

I want goat cheese, unleavened bread, wine . . .
the strong wine of your youth
when grapes grew & grew under the lucky silver moon.

I want to mix your strong wine with water,
drink from your pieced-together desire.

Sledgehammer

this is the work of the hammer: to break us open
with its ring & clang in the cracking earth
in the autumn ache of water spread between hills
in all these yellow trees, in the roots of them
in flesh grown dry

in leaves on water
in the black crow you dreamed pecking
in bones & dust
in love made out of bruises & threats of death
in belly-ripping want
in the tears of sex beneath leaning trees
in the white mist

in galleries of trees misted with the breath of gods
(the thick sky like muscles of underslung jaws)
in the awful crack of bones broken at their centres

this is the work of the hammer: to drive everything together
to join & connect hearts to each other
to shape vision & pound & crack & dismantle
to break everything apart
in search of the pure in flesh grown dry
in bones & dust

My love is strung with the ancient

How do I love thee   thou inward old
son of a bitch   thou self-dried
self-jailed walking grey wall of prison
guntowers & rusted barbwire   thou

inadvertent passer of genes who
gave me this face   this one short leg   this
cowboy walk?   didst the half of me burn as
it passed through thy cock?   didst thou

weaken in the knees?   did the thread of
blood between us vibrate with
these days when I walk by thee   past thee
through thee as if I don't know how

thee hates thine own face   as if
I don't know how an electric razor lets
thee shave by feel & I must ask: Is it true
vampires cannot manipulate mirrors?

I love thee with the rage of the setting
sun in my bones   in the marrow of them   in
their latticed design   in my larynx   in
the timbre of my

hello to everyone but thee   (these
I acknowledge   love thee   but this body
was one of nine accidents)   I love
thee with all the scars of acne   the blackheads —

submerged poison in my flesh   I love thee with
the rage of the setting sun   with
the temperature of cigarette coals   My
love is strung with the ancient

sinews of tyrannosaurs   their extravagantly
muscled hips & perpetual coil-spring
hind legs   their heads of mostly jaws &
teeth   I love you with all

the destruction of hydrogen bombs   the
crushing of metal against guardrails   the
ice that creeps into cells & ruptures as
it thaws

hearthouse
(for my son, Connor)

the heart holds its own heat,
the heart is its own furnace,
its own fuel

you are the house of my heart
from your tiny limbs   to the lengthening
curl of your red-tinged hair   to your eyes
(just like my eyes) when I come home to them
in my mind

(I come home to a pile of gravel
we scraped together, a pile of gravel and
a rough piece of wood for a chimney)

my heart burns & pumps
heat through you & you
reciprocate   your reciprocal

heat floods through me with the clank & thud of old
radiators in the house of my
heart love is the familiar

creak & sigh of expanding pipes as water
changes temperature & circulates
as you circulate

in my veins & the arteries of my mind   you are central
heating the house of my heart

Making the Middle Be

I recall their way of hanging back;
"Go ahead," they'd say. "Go in
and find yourself a place," while they,
meanwhile, stood at the rear or just
outside the door beneath the bare
bulb's buggy glare, folding their arms
across their chests.
         It's a habit
grown, no doubt, from living marginally,
like arriving late and parking by
the shed well away from the front
yard gate, and in no particular
hurry to snag an up-front seat,
content with any old odd
wobbly-limbed chair, or even
standing up shoulder to the door jamb —
of the back door, the side door,
the kitchen door — any door, in fact,
but the front door.
         Not for them,
making spectacles of their joy;
that's what the fiddler was for,
though even he was but a cog
that turned the wheel of their fun
into a spinning blur.
         Not for them,
making rituals of their suffering;
that's what a Christ was for.
No indignity of public pain,
encircled shame, or gawking at one another's
misery. They must have feared
the trap of talk and needed to know
that they could always go aside,

or crawl away with their destiny
like an old dog withdrawing to the wood.

Of course, they knew what they were about:
by sidling into life this way,
they didn't miss as much.
                    Besides,
when there's so much edge, the centre
of a field holds no holy meaning;
going up and down the rows,
planting sets, uprooting roots,
swathing bands of ripened grain,
or fencing in the cows — that's how
they marked their time, post by post
on a periphery.
                    That's how they marked
their space, uncorking a field lunch tea,
and sprawled on a weedy verge from where
they found their place in the land's
topography —
                    they knew that value's rarely
in the middle; it's making the middle be.

North Shore Park

Last night's winter gale
has blown a desert in, dunes
of snow along the sloping cliffs.
In the glare of this expanse

the seaward-facing benches
look ironic, and a red fox,
the only moving thing, scurries
to the woods, away from icy forms

heaved up like crystal beasts.
Spruce bushes stall at a lean,
while uncomprehending cottages
close their plywood eyes.

Winter, it seems, has rung
its piercing note on the rim
of the shattered sea —
left shards of it everywhere.

Far out, beyond such brokenness,
there might be purer tones,
or maybe one could see the place
where shapes of perfect ice are made.

Now would be the time to go,
to walk for miles on ice,
before the spring slashes through
letting flow marine-blue blood,

now, before those others come,
dreamy for sleep-inducing surf,
hot for magic castles.
Oiled for summer, screened for sun,

they will reconfigure all this ice
to sand, make an oasis here
beneath the tilting pines. Yet the truth
of it may be clearer now —
when the galloping blasts of wind
hoof it in over the frozen Gulf.

from **The Story of My Land**

IV

Birth Story

It was cropping time the night
that I was born. I'm told that you
came home from town to plow the field
above the road. The neighbours must
have seen the tractor's one bright eye
or heard the motor drifting down
the wind. In any case, by morning,
all the stubble lay in folded
rows, and sheets of reddish sod
were steaming wet; an oily spectrum
glistened where the blades had sheared
the brickish clay.
                  Perhaps that's why
I'm closer to the land than some
I know who seem to be of air,
the ones whose coats appear to billow
as they walk, the ones who scarcely
touch the earth, as though they move
through life *en pointe*. Their arms appear
to dangle up, their fingers stroking
clouds that I see only good for bringing
rain.
      The heavy drape of Celtic cloth,
no doubt, has kept me downward
eyed and mostly on the ground,
a farmer's son with heavy bones
and brooding brow.
             When I walked
across these fields, my boots became
a muddy mass, and there was so much
digging through the clover and the grass,
the weeding and the hoeing, and so

much time spent going down beyond
the loam to pebbly sand and stubborn
stone that could be broken only
with a crowbar's weighty strike.

There's been some change since then.
I can't imagine men will come
for me the way they came for you
that day when you had finished
with the field — quietly to the kitchen
door; they wondered if you had
the time, perhaps, and would you mind.

The way you placed your shovel
in the truck, and your bar, they knew
they could depend on you, a good
and steady man who knew how wide,
how deep, how well it should be done —
the digging of a neighbour's grave.

Dark Horses

Steady to the end,
the limits of his life
defined by fences, hedges,

headlands in a field,
he chose a day of rest
as if he knew the work

could wait, then sought
final comfort circling
square familiar corners,

sniffing for his brother
dark horse death. We
should pray for such grace,

that bred-in-the-bone
knowing what we're called to,
early on: plowing, poeming,

harvesting the sea. Would
that bareback rider raking
Irish moss at Skinner's Pond

agree? In my dream he clutches
madly at a white-flecked mane.
I wake when the anvil ocean bed

leaps up to meet the surging
sledge of beast and tide.

Cormorants

So. The cormorants have come home
to roost. Crook-necked upright bats,
I thought at first: Pictou Landing,
twenty years ago. Bagpipes balanced
on cabers. Unlikely twisted birds.

Now whole colonies host wherever
web-clawed perch, or purchase,
might be had: a half-sunken pier
at St. Catherine's, the pilings
of long-gone Hillsborough Bridge.

Misshapen blow-ins from over
the Strait. Brine-blackened sticks.
Why would I envy your more-than-
native wingspread ease? Wind-
whipped remnants of tarpaper shacks.

Some Days, Paradise

Some days, Paradise seems just a stone's throw
away; as easy, even, as the *skip,*
skip of a rock, smoothed by the ebb and flow
of rough tides, slung sidearm from a snug grip
across a blinking bay. One perfect fling
might send it skimming to the other side —
or so you like to think, imagining
its last beach-bound *hop* with Olympic pride!
Then how would you stride after it — a god
almost, almost walking on the water . . .
until, brought back to dry land by a *plod,*

plod in the sand — your shore-combing daughter —
you help fill a pail with sea-washed glass, boat-
shaped shells, and pebbles flat enough to float.

A Prayer for My Daughters

Outside another storm is howling; more
terrific than the one a poet heard
so many years ago, this tempest's roar
has loosened like a pickaxe the mortared
brick of faith. No master mason, I shore
up with doubtful timber — knotty, tortured
slabs of dim thought — the burden-bearing wall
of overwrought belief. It may yet fall.

On nights like this I shudder when, resigned
to fitful rest (at best), I rise to gaze
upon seraphic forms. Sprawled in purblind
bliss — so seemingly immune to my malaise —
those shadowy innocents call to mind
pale plaster-cast cherubs psaltering praise
from vaulted heights: rapture in high relief,
keystones rosettes in overarching grief.

Faultless harbingers of redeeming grace,
or heralds of the firmament's collapse?
Against the dark, my smarting eyes retrace
an archived image of nave, transept, apse —
a cathedral's heart — ravaged by the race
of wildfire over oak and stone. Perhaps
the answer lies buried in smoke-stained panes,
a sharded puzzle in rubbled remains.

Faith of my father, assuage my despair!
(Once, he saw in the glinting gilt-framed glass
on a print — *The Holy Family*, I swear —
his infant son falling, a hurtling mass,
and leaping caught him at the bottom stair.)
My daughters! Heaven forbid that I pass
disquiet to you. Pray that I root out
relics of hope from black ruins of doubt.

For Mordecai Richler's Shalinsky Who Said "A Jew Is An Idea"

In the days before
the synagogue's fire   when I was thirteen
I would take such a thought as this
a problem worth a morning's pondering
to the Shul
to the dusty corner next the Ark
where sat Epstein
beneath his grey homburg   *reading*
tucked within the folds of his yellowing Tallith
(a shawl that could canopy a wedding party)
I would go to his seat before opening prayers
and put it all to him   this man
who could love his people no more
if he lived as long again
And I can see old Epstein place his finger
in the book of prayer   close it
and look up
Epstein who was master of a good six tongues
not counting Yiddish and Hebrew
would say   with a confidant's smile
so I could understand
"You know, eh, that the Creator
(whose Name we cannot pronounce)
made the heaven and earth in six days,
and before He rested on the seventh
which he made especially holy, eh, as He should,

You know this? that on the morning of the sixth day
He rubbed the dust between His fingers and said,
and this I tell you now He said, 'You know,
I have got a Wonderful Idea!'"

Aphelion

My father loves with the knuckles
of his words, dottled fists
that cut the air, find
an attenuated target.

On what might be his deathbed
he tries again to force the arc,
and fails,
        for once,
to complete the bony kiss.

Such effort sends a weary man,
however resolute,
              tilting into his age,
to go on tilting,
long after I've abandoned him
to himself.

My Father Plaits His Granddaughter's Hair

From the unfathoming of his sickbed,
something in my father has found
the August rope of my daughter's hair,
and slowly, painfully,
his chill fingers begin to climb.

Not a mime's device
or the mocking of a fairy tale,
but the work of some old *fakir*.

I can believe, for the moment,
that he might rise from his pillows
and this sea-spider's web
of shiny tubing, that
my daughter, angled over him,
between sea and sky
like some golden verb,
might draw him through to the surface.

Something in my father, her grandfather,
something secret,
                    finds its name, then,
determined to live.

And he, this once, decides
not to argue.

The muted

The muted *pluck, pluck* of the embroiderer's needle
through taut linen — an octave higher,
they would be raindrops in green abandoned ponds.
Schools are needed for these superior altitudes.

The silence is ready, but a science of silence
is not yet in place, although in this context
a candlewick crumbling in the steady exhalation of its flame
is often heard. A state subsidy might be offered

if the state were not obsessed with the one
needful thing, its own perpetuation.
The women's hands are clusters of arpeggios.

But the mind that dreams behind them and emerges
at their touch is a greater wonder yet.
The darkness is suddenly all wings and then dawn.

You Wanted to Hear

You wanted to hear angels sing — to render audible
the mystery that each voice goes a journey of its own
while together they make one will, one end. Here meanwhile
at the other extremity of things, rain beats for centuries

on thin walls, and a woman bends at a lonely instrument. You too,
if you listen with self-surrender, will hear between her hands'
encounters with the strings a drop that falls forever and never
strikes a stone. "Joy is easy," sing your orphan girls, "charity and clarity

of spirit, near and now." The woman whose fingers step for me
so lingeringly opens an uncompromising emptiness.
There are mountains in my country as in yours, standing

with their snows above cities floating in image on water
by the winter light of old paintings. Walking today together
where the fortress once stood, I hear, faint yet sure, another, a new

music neither yours nor mine, deep within, high in the air.

Early Morning Was

Early morning was Japanese. You could feel the faintly
oatish grain of the paper against your skin. Now fog
has lifted, and beads of rain on the leaves have begun to dry.
Red oaks have taken to rustling, and the garden,

spotted with soft-focus blossoms of sunlight, is beautiful still
but less Japanese. The day shift is on at the Toyota works,
and the monks have become invisible. A special zigzag
headtrip up the watersteps once held the arrangement together.

Now new principles of organization are retraining admirers
to accomplish a comparable stitchery — not forgetting
the old way of stopping on the bridge in a place shifted

by a few inches back or forth from day to day to extract
all values of the variables. How soon it has come to be evening,
and cries of blackbirds from the sedges acquire an undertone

close to a dry brush's rasp on laid paper. What could be monks
coaching unidentifiable apprentices are tending the garden.

All Light

All light is fossil light. It says the earliest moments of a star,
the default of a primary civilization. It fixes the specimen in eternity.
You can saw the petrified log later and polish its cross-section
to art, science, religion, boredom. Or not. The signals

may never get picked up by any other atom. On the other hand, the
    spin-flip
of one of a practically unaddable set of orbiting events may catch the
    eye
and have a museum built around it. The palaeozoic sea floor
sticks to your shoes in wet weather and leaves traces everywhere.

No food is wasted. The eaters scurry in, bristly with self-importance,
to get it, or it relaxes into something inedible but just as useful.
Most of the others seem to know exactly what they want, even though

they've never encountered it; you yourself are almost always unsure.
The structure of populations constantly alters. The species
that forage a given climatic province are trial

translations of a yet-to-be-accomplished animal design.

How Could They

How could they be anything but elegies, those stories
of love between mortals and immortals? How can he but
obey and die when, seizing him reluctant by the hair,
she draws back his head, exposing to the approaching spear

that soft place where the neck throbs and armour does not reach?
How can she not shed tears, though destined to live

for ever and forget her mortal son, to see him at her knees
begging as when he was a child to have lights among the branches

lit once more, though tomorrow, as both know,
he will be dragged to death under chariot wheels?
These stars in this sky forget briefly how not to shine.

After their moment, there's nowhere to read them from. A few
fraying threads hold the book together. Already wind is turning
     pages
faster than you can see to remember even the most impassioned
     words.

The unicorn

Potentiality collapses into fact, the wave
function submits to an act of registration,
and a field wide as the world unfolds. Yet never
a trackless waste. Every time the field comes supplied

with an angelhead of whisperishly branching paths
by which he finds election, choosing at each remove,
by scent of flowers and grasses, among the many
ways to go. He will end by a lake or in a brimming

sunny clearing on a summer's day. Don't be surprised
if, inspired by intentionality to gather salad herbs,
you find him on your threshold as you open the garden door,
a wanderer from a distant era of romance, pausing briefly

before rededication to the flux of time. Inspection
of the relevant equations confirms him as a possible
solution, once his characterizing boundary conditions
have been discerned and put in place. Given those synthetic

a priori determinations, he will appear necessary and irrefutable.
Damp them out, and he dissolves again into the rampant and
    omnipotent
evolutionary ocean of unspecified and unappeasable desire.

NEWFOUNDLAND

What's Lost

The Labrador coastline is a spill of islands,
salt-shaker tumble of stone,
a cartographer's nightmare —
on the coastal boat 50 years ago
the third mate marked his location after dark
by the outline of a headland against the stars,
the sweetly acrid smell of bakeapples blowing off
a stretch of bog to port or starboard,
navigating without map or compass
where hidden shoals shadow the islands
like the noise of hammers echoed across a valley.

The largest are home to harbours and coves,
a fringe of clapboard houses
threaded by dirt road,
grey-fenced cemeteries sinking
unevenly into mossy grass.
Even those too small to be found on the map
once carried a name in someone's mind,
a splinter of local history —
a boat wracked up in a gale of wind,
the roof-wrecked remains of a stage house
hunkered in the lee.

Most of what I want him to remember
lies among those islands, among the maze
of granite rippling north a thousand miles,
and what he remembers is all I have a claim to.
My father nods toward the coastline,
to the bald stone shoals almost as old as light —
That was 50 years ago, he says,
as a warning, wanting me to understand
that what's forgotten is lost
and most of this he cannot even recall
forgetting

Capelin Scull

What you'd imagine the sound of
an orchestra tuning up might look like,
cacophony of sliver and black at your feet.
Spawning capelin washed onto
grey sand beaches in the hundreds
of thousands like survivors of a shipwreck,
their furious panic exhausted into
helpless writhing while boys scoop them
into buckets with dip-nets.
They migrate all the way
from the Caribbean for this,
each wave rolling onto the shore
like another bus stuffed with
passengers bound for oblivion,
limbs and heads hanging recklessly
through the open windows.

Most of them rotted on the beach
or found their way onto gardens
planted with potatoes in those days,
except for the few we dried on
window screens beside the shed,
neat rows of the tiny fish
endlessly buzzed over by houseflies
like crazy eighth notes on a staff.
Roasted them over open flame
until they were black and they tasted
much as you'd imagine burnt fish would
but we ate them anyway
head and tail together.
They had come such a long way
and given themselves up so completely
and in such an awful silence
that we felt obliged to
acquire the taste.

Painting the Islands

At first glance the coast of islands
is treeless, a monochrome beige or grey,
the hills in the distance flayed
or worn smooth like a whetstone worked by a knife.
Narrow valleys of green emerge from shadow
as you sail into them,
stands of dwarf spruce in thin soil,
their roots tendrilled to stone;
white antlers of snow glitter in high crevices,
meadows of moss cover the sway-backed headlands
clean as a freshly mown lawn.
In the brief three months of a northern summer
fields of white heather and honeysuckle
find grace enough to bloom,
bushels of blueberries ripen
in the wet of August rain.

To paint the islands properly
you have to see them up close,
to know the light that inhabits their darkness —
moments of rust and bronze in
the dull granite rock,
the Neopolitan swirl of molten lava
fissured through the grain of hillsides.

Approaching Nain, the islands
are bare and burnished black,
metallic glint of the afternoon sun
caught by long blades of mica
imbedded in the surface
and for the few minutes it takes
to sail beyond them the stones
are alive with light.

Loom
Burnt Woods Cemetery, Western Bay, Newfoundland

The meadow grass hemming
the gravesites is coarse as raw wool,
thickets of dry thistle
stand like needles clustered
in a pincushion; overhead
a shoddy bolt of cloud
gone ragged at the edges.

Headstones facing the Atlantic
set in rows like figures being
fitted by a tailor;
six feet beneath them
the remains of the cloth I was cut from,
the patterns lifted to cobble
my features together.

Such a slow undressing —
bones divested of flesh,
purposeless and absurd,
like a dressmaker's dummy
relegated to the basement;
skulls hollow as thimbles,
picked clean of every thread
of memory, design.

They were born into times
when you made do,
stitched trousers out of burlap sacking,
salvaged skirts from a wreck
of worn curtains,
when there was no disguising
most of a life comes to us piecemeal,
second-hand.

Even the love I bear these strangers
is makeshift, threadbare,
fashioned by necessity.
The bitter cold draws thin gloves
of blood to my hands
and I follow the footpath
weaving among their graves
as long as I can stand the keen,
surrender them finally to the wind
shearing in off the endless
grey loom of the sea.

Burn

1

When the salt water burns —
Cities tumbling pillars in
Sheets of flame on the water —
It's sure to be a south wind
And massing thick with fish.

2

A thin line a good salter walks —
Salt his man or his master.
Not enough salt makes the fish greasy,
Slippery, too slimy to dry.
Too much salt burns up the fish —
All brittle when it comes to dry.

3

Nothing in him but bung-your-eye —
He walked ten miles in the blizzard —
The frost burnt his toes —
Thawed by the fire, they
Mortified so far that off came
The nails, and bared the ends of his bones.
And all he could talk of was the kentals of cod.

The Marriage

Bridesboys

Sudden as a northeasterly,
The engagement.
Up and down the harbour, the six of us,
Bidding the neighbours, *come to the wedding*.
Now, we come up with moonshine galore —
Oh yes, more than we bargained for —
My son, we all had a fine jag on.
A racket out on the bridge —
Up she went like a brindy bough,
And the father, stiff as brewis,
Come out and drove us off out of it,
And the water barrels upsot, the
Bride cake made away with.
The day after, a big kick-up.
We were all mops and brooms.
Small chance he'll have us in for a
Bite of the groaning cake,
Come the fall.

First Boat

Eyes like the cornflower. And a
Real devil-ma-click —
I knew when I married him.
First boat on the water —
"Where's that sun to,
Lollygagging about?" he'd grin
On his way out the door.
Ours the highest woodstack.
Ours the stable stuffed with hay.
Our goats the fattest.
Our quilts the most rumpled.
He'd ruffle my hair,

Grin, "Where's that sun to,
Lollygagging about?"
Our sweat on his shoulders.
His blue eyes blazing.

The Cross-handed Bed

She was a bit of a woman —
A waist like a wasp when I married her,
But strong — no one could beat her for work —
Six loaves every day and the
Wash out on the line
Before the sun rose on the water.
She sang like the wren.
Up at the window when our boat came in.
She welcomed
Each youngster that came —
But the ninth torn her open.
Now she's in the ground
Our old four-poster's all reefs and sunkers
And I'm bound out for Wareham's
In search of a cross-handed bed.

TOM DAWE

Abandoned Outport

Sun on boarded windows
and gull cries
high in the August clouds.

On a small beach path:
bluebells nodding
over driftwood.

A bee is buzzing
inside dark cracks
in a windowpane.

Clover meadow:
above the rusting ploughshare
a butterfly.

A sudden fog
and sea winds
bend the sting nettle.

Deep in graveyard grass
snails and lichens
cling to the headstone.

Across the schoolhouse floor:
paper scraps, dry seaweed
and a dead moth.

Against the cold twilight:
dark picket fences
and a crow's flight.

In a rising moon:
a church steeple
and lilac leaves.

If Sonnets Were in Fashion

If sonnets were in fashion,
I think I would try one
about a dog I heard
barking one time
in a taped poetry reading
by Robert Frost.
The imagery would be geological
and the old man of fire and ice,
plain diction, the gravel voice
could have the octave
all to himself,
free to be crafty
yet seeming so undesigning
within the confines
of iambic walls,
his presentation glacial, powerful,
moving on the slow import
of its melting. . . .
And then, intruding into line eight,
in a tree-at-my-window pause,
that audible fossil,
just for a couple of seconds,
a dog barking faintly somewhere.

The creature would have the sestet
all to itself,
so perfectly autonomous out there
in pussy-willow swamp
and prime New England sunshine,
casually scanning its territory,
cocking its leg
against the world perhaps,
its primitive spondee
lingering and wonderful.
Oblivious to any

iamb or anapest,
it would just be
its own wild poetry,
a summons
from the wordless places
once again.

Daedalus

Alone on the beach this morning
I catch myself
blaming the gods again
for this poised gull
against the sky,
mocking me now
as they did once
at my son's funeral
when a partridge laughed
from somewhere
in the grove.
I dream that day back
with gentle sea swell,
goats, green island,
the lip of a grave,
and sorrow planting me
like some tree
twisted
in sea wind.

On morning wings
across the sun
he comes before me,
there at the seabird's core,

my son,
the slave girl's child,
that shadowy
all-too-human form,
five-pointed man
inside translucent feather.
Cruel are those gods
who coax
with sunshine!

Now I am forced
to see him
falling
once more,
clawing
the air
so far
beyond
my pleading.
And as he goes
by me,
one last
glimpse
of the slave
girl
free somehow
in frightened
contours
of his face.
And the mesmerizing
space
of it all,
the small flag
of a foot
disappearing
into the shimmer
of the herring
shoals.

And far away,
as if they know
about it already,
waiting, nodding,
placed there
for my returning,
sinewy, sunburned men,
like a chorus
of cormorants,
picking their snarled nets
along a seawall,
voicing their platitudes
against all heedless youth;
the mesh of an old hubris
closing in again.

Riddle

I see them in summer
twilight,
six or seven sitting in a kitchen.
The lights are not on yet
and my father comes
in through the door
from the day's cod-splitting.
Behind him the horns of a new moon
rise up from a cloud bank.
The tide is pulsing
up the ladders of a stage head.
Cleansed by an afternoon
of blood
and salt-spilling,
father is straight and tall,

joking as he takes the beams
on his shoulders
and joins the others
in a riddle spell.

Patient as anchor rust,
he awaits his turn
before he offers:
"What goes over the water,
and under the water,
without touching the water?"
In the pause,
the sea whispers.
Then grandfather answers:
"An egg in a duck's belly."

My mother,
six weeks married,
smiles coyly
in a corner.
Much against their wishes,
she has been swimming
all by herself
again this afternoon
over on Swan Island.
She has not told anybody yet
that she is expecting me.

Utopia

I

An immense acreage of solitude.
No one has lived here
Or left more than a shadow
Among shrubs and stones.
The hill falls to water
And a carious rock:
Geology is a study of the spirit,
One place forming another
In the migrations of a continent.
I am always here
On a hillside of quartz and juniper,
A ridge over water
Where the whales blow and dive,
And the grounded icebergs topple
In a smoke of gulls.
This place is twenty years of me,
The stark coastland of a question.

II

Who dares learn such emptiness,
Contending with thoughts of ocean,
Or interiors yet a wilderness?
And learning, who dares forget?
The world is more populous than the soul:
There are hermits in Soho.
Europe will have a radioactive Summer
And tumours subsequently.
This morning as I prayed
Americans flew past in a transport plane
Perhaps too full of bombs for greeting.

I listen to my breath
And the machine that eats motor cars
For breakfast;
They find nutrition in our old manoeuvres.
I am still listening to my breath,
I think that I am here.

III (Isaiah 22:16-18)

What right have you here,
And what relatives have you here
For you to hew yourself
A tomb in this place?
See, Yahweh hurls you down,
Down with a single throw;
Then with a strong grip he grips you
And winds you up into a ball
And hurls you into an immense country.
There you will die.

IV

O my immense country of no place,
There is nowhere as strange as now.
I am alone in this acreage of breath,
Landscape of spruce, fir, clover, and rock,
A lifetime expiring somewhere worlds away.

Crossing the Straits

The sea is moving under our passage,
An old year out and a new year in
Between Port aux Basques and North Sydney.
The ship rolls in the first breaths of a gale;
It has been so long, ten or twelve years,
Since I last sailed, I do not trust my legs
Or stomach to hold against the weather,
So lie still as a narrow berth allows,
Reminding myself that disaster
Is a kind of lottery, and to sink
As hard as winning millions on dry land,
And that sailors, having made profession
Of storms, know their work and die old.
In an hour, anxiety drowns in sleep;
The mind, as ever, opposes passage,
And I dream of my flat in Toronto,
Its wooden deck stretching across the roof,
A ship remote from this night's turning.
At six I wake and walk through lounges
Where some have sat up all night playing cards
Or talking, their New Year's revels queasy
And circumspect where the ship's movement
Began the hangovers before the drinks.
More have slept in the rows of La-Z-Boys
Before an almost bloodshot TV screen,
Its hoarse voice still croaking festively
About the crowds that gathered in Times Square.
The gales have subsided and the sea is calm
Less than an hour out of North Sydney;
A heavy breakfast later, I walk along
A deck where snow-crusted lifeboats are hung.
I imagine that in summer this is
The ship's best place, but the air is frigid
This morning, and Newfoundlanders crossing
The Straits see water enough in warmer times
To forego the prospect now, but this moment

Of pent chances, between home and home,
Is not mine alone, and for most who travel
There is some tear in memory between
The longed for and the given, what they left
And what they are. Nova Scotia looms,
And the purser summons drivers to cars
In the ship's belly, where the tractor-trailers
Are already roaring for landfall.

Tropical Toads

They're big for toads, lumpy,
soft as baseball gloves left out
in the rain. Still, they're not so easy to
see on steps in the dark or squatting near
stopped-up drains. They'll sit for hours,
unblinking, monks in the smoky light,
unperturbed by the passing world.

Single-minded, it's *equanimitas*
they're after, toad-soul hovering somewhere
window-high but leaving the warted corpse
behind, shadows in shadows and catastrophic
for careless walkers, brooders, dreamers,
lovers going up from the beach, eye-locked
and barefoot. They're the drunk's worst
fear in the tropical night, the cause of brilliant
leaps and dodges, world-class tumbles,
torn ligaments and some wonderful
lies in the morning.

Or as lovers, they're contemplative, cautious,
eschewing the bright flame, the Italian
passion. They'll drive you mad,
pledging their constancy, croaking
all night under your balcony. And they're
deadly, the people tell you, toxic if you
eat one. You wonder what they think you
had in mind, or how they know
as loose dogs know: a dog might
sniff at a toad from behind, give
it a nudge to see what happens,
the toad might hop an inch or
two but that's about it.
He won't be worried from his dreams.

It's an odd defense in a sudden, unsubtle
country, a kind of after-the-fact retaliation.
But clearly the word's got around.
And there's something decent about it,
tidy too, knowing the one you got
was the one you wanted.

They're different from things that
creep up walls and crawl into shadows,
not so frantic to stab, sting, bite, disembowel
or suck your blood. They're a lovely kind
of deadly creature, tropical toads,
you can get quite foolish about them,
so long as you send your friends
ahead in the night
and forget about the moon.

Night Crossing in Ice

We locked the cars and looked at the sea,
grey and empty, nothing like inland ponds and lakes
we knew. The close cloud. Wreckage and rock.
The start or end of things who could say?

We went aboard the *William Carson* in the dark,
the wind's kiss like a lost wife. Gulls looked away
as we sailed. Nine or ten hours the crossing
if the weather holds but we barely get into
the bar when the fun begins
pitch and roll and
bang. Jesus Christ the bow riding up
and hammering down we grab at anything,
lifted and dangled, our bodies hopeless, knowing nothing

of this rhythm. *Porpoising, boys, that's what we calls it.*
Guaranteed she'll be a memorable night.

Who could call this heaving darkness home?
Who'd leave his house just to watch a game of hockey?
All night a metal door slams shut like someone
looking for the one way out. Up and
pause on the crest and
down with a bang and bang that
bloody door, then deep in the night a grinding inches
from my ear as if we're into a depth of animals. *Nothin but ice*
my love, said a passing voice in the corridor, *pans and a bit of slob,*
we sees all we wants of that in the spring.

Signal Hill

Marconi, of course, and the whisper
from Poldhu. The wind stirs awake, shaking
the latch. *Too late, cock* — the S caught like a spark
in the brilliant kite above the fever hut on the land's
last hill. Half Irish, he would have appreciated
the ironies. The room's crowded, reeking of wet coats
and excitement. *Tell us what this means.*
An elegant man, he draws a hand through the air
as if to demonstrate the absence of wires.

And who's in the crowd? Ned Pratt for one
who, later, living in Toronto, would count the left turns
across traffic before he'd agree to go anywhere.
Yet spread the word he would until the end:
Tarpaulins ripped. Another hatch let go . . .
Where are you, "Antinoe?"

But what about these, the S's, O's and J's
that flash from the rocks and ruined guns?
K.G. from Key West. Ron and Shaky here in '84
SAVE THE WHALES!! Indonesians out of East Timor!!!
And all the lovers staking claims, as fierce as traders
at the stock exchange: *Lefty loves Madonna.*
Carla and J. Wolfe. And down by the tide line,
boldly, where the seaweed slaps and tosses like a lover's hair,
Patrick and Sandy 4 ever, and closer, where the footing's
surer, *Patrick and Fran.*

Signals all.
The homes on ledges with patches of lawn,
symmetrical pots on steps. Fish kites. Chinese lights.
Fencefuls of wind toys meant to joke the wind around.

Signals every one.
As surely as the winking lights
in the rocks. Halfway back from the harbour,
the walkway spans a cut in the rock where the air
hangs cool and rank. Pigeons whirr and flap,
climbing into the light from nests on narrow ledges. Something
breathes below, splashes and coughs. Something
taking its own good time.

Ah, but the lovers the lovers who
climb over boulders and dangle four-fingered
from trestles. Darkness won't stop them,
decrees, or disapproving strollers, the passing pairs
of older women with blue hair and blood-coloured nails,
walking the government walkways,
holding the government rails.

Let Us Go and Find a Place of Worship

At a quarter to eleven
on an ordinary Wednesday
the church bells have been ringing
clear in the clarion-carrying air
for five full minutes —
what is this,
another death or what is going on?

Above the houses across the street
fawn-coloured branches scratch
stiffly, arthritically
at pigeon-coloured clouds,
try to scrape them
off the blue beyond, the hidden
sky over sky.

Keep the taps running, you said:
this recent rain has merely driven
the frost deeper underground;
two hundred households have awakened
to empty pipes singing the absence of water.

Veering toward St. Patrick's Church,
two ancient women are walking uphill,
their backs bent to hold the grade inside themselves
as balance. Thick, I wonder how
they can walk on legs as slim as twigs
and still hold that hill
so placidly inside their hips.

I hear your breath
between the peals of bells —
almost in hibernation, your sleeping voice
occupies the space between weekday pilgrims' steps.

You say you have no need for these sharp mornings,
for revelations to rouse you.

But let us go and find
a place of worship; something is stirring,
perhaps the groundbreaking of the spring
echoing through basements, or the tremor
that shakes the dormancy of seeds, wakes
them from a dream of their own brief flowering.

I wish you could hear yourself.
In the room where you wait
this frozen season out,
your every breath is a longing for summer.

Solar Eclipse, St. John's, Newfoundland

The whole city strains, the tension
of not looking at the sun
is palpably too much: something like a great groan
is heard from yards and alleys
as eyes are pulled away.

Here in this grey border town, border to Atlantis,
city of shipwrecks, city of the drowned, the sun
draws up the sea and makes sky of it:
today, long lines of evaporation
like images from cheap Resurrection pictures
tug at the heartstrings and optic nerves.

On Water Street, still running rivulets from yesterday,
a man says to his buddy, "Don't go lookin' at it!
It'll blind your eyes." And his buddy says, "Ah, boy,
I mightn't see it again anyway til August."

What to gamble? City of ironies and things too wet to iron:
Might admiring the sun mean never seeing it again?
It sounds like something that could happen where
the solar eclipse yields that miracle —
the brightest day in two weeks.

Booman

Beware the shadowy booman in the evening garden,
a spectre from the years the grass grew high
as houses. Beware the moment when light is unsure.
There he'll be waiting,
all smoke and shadow and shimmer-shape.
With the crook of his finger, he'll beckon you over
'cross the crimped summer hay he'll call you, say
"My, you're after getting some nice fat legs.
My, what a grand big girl."
Once he appeared in a cellar door;
he was not there a second before.
His face wavered in the heat haze
and it was not night, but the burnished
centre of an August day.
I caught his gaze upon my scrawny shape
like a small, chill wind from nowhere,
rising and teasing and falling,
all in a moment, and gone.
The booman waited, found me late
at night on a city street
where trees were thick and crowds thin,
tried to frig me, frighten me
but I got away with loud curses,
the pump of my grand girl's legs. I still expect him
some nights on some streets

where the dark lies heavy and sweet and deep
as the grass where I first found him.
The best protection is to never discount him.

How to Leave an Island

             with alacrity
is one way:
speeding for the silver tube of plane,
you become it, aerodynamo, windborne;
grow aeroshell, revise your lungs
for a leap into space. For a moment you will see
the island cartographic; for the first time
you will disappear from a map.

             with a song in your heart
is another way:
you recall a scene from a movie, the last
night of love; the lover rushes naked
to a waiting car, speeds, top down,
mist on naked flesh; you are that lover,
the song plucked on the strings of your nerves,
impossible to sing, despair and joy.

             syllable by syllable
is another way:
waking you find you speak a different language;
in a long dream, the vernacular has evaporated
from your body like the long fogs of June leaving,
and when the woman at the crosswalk notes *sun shower*,
you have no memory. The way she looks at you
when you mutter, *O, Amon-Re, even the sun rains here*.

                    molecule by molecule
is another way:
perched on a cliff you feel your body disappear
cell by corpuscle; your useless hands can launch
no boat, nor skyward thing. Around you gulls wheel,
drop spiny urchin shells; Daedalus by default, Icarus
under construction, high on the aerie of a dream, staring
at a banned ocean, poised on the very edge of flight.

Another Night in Crawley's Cove

The accordion considers the tunes it knows best.
The conversation, though incoherent, is congenial.

Outside, the balsams are dancing in the wind.
(The branches, an orchestra of castanets.)
Somewhere in the sky, the birds are sound asleep.

The giddy dancers are stepping it out
on the floorboards of their spindrift dreams.

Tomorrow, the music will be still, the sky quiet
and the birds will be back in the backyard woods.

The day will pass without measure until
night falls and time begins again. The birds
will take to the sky, the dreamers to their feet
and the floor will endure or enjoy another night
of jigs, reels, knee-slapping yarns, out-of-tune
tunes and foot-stomping songs.

Elsewhere in the cove there are people asleep.
They'll be up and about before dawn, long before
the last lie has been told and we've all gone
to rest in peace.

The old Waterford wood stove has grown cold.
But there's no discomfort here in this elderly house
on the hill. We are contentedly tired and ready
to creep or crawl to our makeshift beds to await
this day's dawning.

The water, lapping at the landwash, will lull us
to sleep until the birds in the balsams wake us
to another day in Crawley's Cove and another night

close to the floor, well removed from the lives
we live when here is far away. And we are elsewhere.

Where we are the most we have of ourselves.
And the least we have of each other.

Lupines
   (for Frieda)

Across the ditch by the graveyard fence
a groundbound rainbow of purple and pink.

Triumphant yesterday in the Trinity Bay sun.
Courageously upright today
in this day's torrential downpour.

I come upon them suddenly
at a quick twist in the twisted road.
Whatever the weather, they are here
this summer season like a bright ribbon
of light, not quite, but almost
out of sight.

Behind and above them, sleeping deep
in the rainsoaked earth, the dead rest
deep in peace.

Below, the waves wash
in their eternal turn upon
the Goose Cove shore.

Making my way to Trinity
in this morning's morning deluge
(soaked to the skin and bereft of love)

I would tip my hat to the trinity
of the sea, the dear departed
and the lupines blooming between.

I don't happen to have a hat on my head
but I do wear a prayer in my heart.

I make a secret Sign of the Cross
and say silently inside to the one god
who doesn't believe in me, "God bless
the long and just gone dead, the sullen
slate-grey sea, and especially (now)
I pray, please bless the lupines blooming there
upright (purple, pink) and right as rain.

Drowned

He saw the bloated mess
under the wharf.
He walked to the house directly,
told everyone to stay away,
had a shot of black rum
he'd saved for Christmas
and went looking for men
and a tarp.

> Women stand in doorways
> or about the slope
> with one arm holding sweaters
> around their shoulders;
> the other holding future fishermen
> closer to their thighs.

On the Ice

We were the first steamer in the fat that spring.
A man from Bay D'Espoir slipped going over the
side; and however it was he took the steel, he
snapped his back and died without a sound. In the
forward hold, we put him on ice and salted him down.

(When we docked in St. John's, we shipped him home
in a coastal boat and, out of consideration for the
poor bugger's family, we sent along his share of
the voyage. Y'know, he went with more money than
the rest of us, for his share wasn't cropped by the
cost of grub or the price of his berth.)

White Wedding

Before a heaping, steaming breakfast was delivered
    to the newlyweds, their first loving;

before they left the hearty celebration downstairs:
    abandoned jackets, rolled sleeves,
    cards and cuffers;

before the mouth organ commanded the feet,
    the table of the wedding feast;

before switchel made invisible rounds,
    the minister drank his lime drink,
    took his leave;

before hurrying from church to house through new snow,
    church doors opened and the light
    struck out, bold as flesh;

before they stood before the altar, she watched
    moonrise — early, lonely, faraway —
    heard bells ring all
    to the ceremony;

before all this, he cleared a path to the church,
    fired up the stoves inside,
    set a diamond of light
    into each gilded lantern
    of the church's chandeliers.

    Now, very late, they hold
    the curtain back
    to watch guests carry
    lanterns and laughter
    out into the winter night;

they stand for a moment
in a common glow,
then scatter the island
with atoms of light.

The Laboratory

The laboratory: long low building wide windows.
I kept it under construction always; when an
old wing was torn down, I ordered a new wing
framed up — always work in progress. Inside,
there never was a ceiling. Wires dangled from
the rafters like nerve ends. The workbenches
against the walls were burdened with heavy
contraptions or decorated with intricate airy
structures made of glass tubing, flasks and
beakers. My inventors stood by windows and
held parts to light to examine them for function
or flaw. Other times they hunched over machines
shaping and shaving metal, leaving the floor
littered with shiny spirals that curved the edge
of light that lined through the imperfectly
joined seams, light that sometimes bent through
flasks of coloured chemicals and made visible
metallic dust that clogged the air; a small
iron furnace added smells and smoke that burned
the throat and the floor of the laboratory was
cluttered enough: massive black batteries, cogs,
levers, tools of heavy iron, magnetic coils,
galvanometers, condensers, tuning forks, iron
bars, pumps wheezing lung-like and things always
thudding or shattering on the floor. In the
centre of it all: the glassblower with his

puffed cheeks and slow-spin pipe; he blew globes
of light wonder, ready to float away. Always
the possibility, or discovery, or event. The
atmosphere expectant — once a blue electric
bolt jumped the length of the lab and cleansed
the air just like that. Notions ricocheted off
all things and stood odd-angled to one another
in freely-formed compositions. Absently, I'd
open a door to a demolished wing and find myself
on a threshold of light and air facing the
meadow — a stunning tangent to it all.

from *The Grey Islands*

"They all save one last squirt"

they all save one last squirt
till they're clear of the water,
black splats straight in the air,
up your sleeve, into your eye.

we sit tossing our jiggers,
ducking, chuckling, piling up squids
easy as pie.

"Take a chunk outa ya big as a dime,"
Nels says, shaking one down that's
braided around his arm.

"Fall in there and they'd drown ya,
drag ya down."

dark in the water long forms shoot crisscross
like limbs of a sunken forest. strange.
not the same things we're pulling in,
stringy legs, flabby pouches.

coming up they ink wildly, puff like
parachutes. trying to put on the brakes.

dying they make small sunsets
with their bodies. glow blood-orange, freckle
like trout, huff, sigh. drain iridescent
green. lemon. white.

"Dry 'em on a line," Nels says. "Wintertime,
put 'em in a toaster same as a slice a bread.
Sure! Better'n potato chips!"

Cedar Cove

If your wharf is washed away
it will come to Cedar Cove —
Wild Cove on the maps or
Capelin Cove. If your boat

goes down it will sail to Cedar
Cove piece by piece.
And your uncle, should he not come back
from his walk on Cape St. George,

will be found grinning among
the glitter of barkless roots
laths struts stays
stringers and frayed rope

in Cedar Cove, where no
cedars have ever grown,
but that's what the local people
call it. The water horizon

topples straight down
on Cedar Cove over
and over, box cars
falling, loads of TNT.

And the wind will not let you speak
in Cedar Cove, which could
be called Deaf Cove
or Lobotomy Cove, will not

let you think or stand straight;
the shrunk trees writhe
and have the wrong kinds
of leaves, but their roots spread

wide in Cedar Cove,
whose gravel is soft compared

to its air. We have come to Cedar
Cove overland, my love

and I, having been lost
at sea in another way.
All day we scatter
ourselves through the noise

and whiteness, learning the thousand
ways things can be taken
apart and reassigned —
the boot sole impaled on the shattered

trunk, the rust flakes,
the bone flakes encrusting a bracelet
of kelp — losing our pictures
of home, stick by stick.

After Cedar Cove,
how will we look?

That Night We Were Ravenous

Driving from Stephenville in the late October
dusk — the road swooping and disappearing ahead
like an owl, the hills no longer playing dead
the way they do in the daytime, but sticking their black
blurry arses up in the drizzle and shaking themselves,
heaving themselves up for another night of
leapfrog and Sumo ballet — some

trees detached themselves from the shaggy
shoulder and stepped in front of the car. I swerved

through a grove of legs startled by pavement, maybe a
hunchbacked horse with goitre, maybe a team of beavers
trying to operate stilts: it was the

landscape doing a moose, a cow
moose,
most improbable forest device. She danced
over the roof of our car in moccasins.

She had burst from the zoo of our dreams and was
there, like a yanked-out tooth the dentist
puts in your hand.

She flickered on and off.
She was strong as the Bible and as full of lives.
Her eyes were like Halley's Comet, like factory whistles,
like bargain hunters, like shy kids.

No man had touched her or given her movements geometry.

She surfaced in front of us like a coelacanth, like a face
in a dark lagoon. She made us feel blessed.

She made us talk like a cage of canaries.

She reminded us. She was the ocean wearing a fur suit.

She had never eaten from a dish.
She knew nothing of corners or doorways.

She was our deaths come briefly forward to say hello.

She was completely undressed.

She was more part of the forest than any tree.
She was made of trees. The beauty of her face was bred
in the kingdom of rocks.

I had seen her long ago in the Dunlop Observatory.

She leapt from peak to peak like events in a ballad.

She was as insubstantial as smoke.

She was a mother wearing a brown sweater opening her arms.

She was a drunk logger on Yonge Street.

She was the Prime Minister. She had granted us a tiny reserve.

She could remember a glacier where she was standing.

She was a plot of earth shaped like the island of
Newfoundland and able to fly, spring down in the middle of
cities scattering traffic, ride elevators, press pop-eyed
executives to the wall.

She was charged with the power of Churchill Falls.

She was a high-explosive bomb loaded with bones and meat.
She broke the sod in our heads like a plough parting the
earth's black lips.

She pulled our zippers down.

She was a spirit.

She was Newfoundland held in a dam. If we had touched her,
she would've burst through our windshield in a wall of blood.

That night we were ravenous. We talked, gulping, waving our
forks. We entered one another like animals entering woods.

That night we slept deeper than ever.

Our dreams bounded after her like excited hounds.

Night in the Ashes

Underneath this blanket of snow,
pressed wildflowers push the white crust.
Last night in the still, I heard them
turn and groan as the stars fell.

Everyone rushed inside to dance
to the accordion and the electric piano —
except for the shell-shocked veterans who stood
leaning into the aluminum siding,
tams pushed back, cigarettes sucked brown,
they twitched and stuttered a history.

When the council bulldozed
the Quonset huts in Kelly's alley,
the youngsters waiting with BB guns and forks
to kill the rats.
"Just don't go in the place," Mom warned.
"The Yanks might have money,
but they also have cockroaches."

I got a french fry cutter and TV rabbit ears
from the shambles of Americana.

We're on the same latitude as northern France;
the sky dissolved like a blotted watercolour,
drops of mauve discolour my arm,
Monet sunsets run into my face.

Somewhere, between dreams and disaster,
children smoke cigarettes
and pencil beards on Queen Elizabeth.
Pigeons gnaw Mary Brown's chicken bones
and yet another person
crucifies the St. Anne's Reel.

I douse the candle,
turn onto my left side
and, finally,
yawn.

The Time That Passes

The time that passes between my mother and me
is more measured in what's not said,
and plain words are felt like samplings of fabrics.

Body, she said, we never said body then,
it was too bold, we said system:
tell the doctor what part of your system hurts.

I linger,
hold onto the feel,
the rub in the mind.

If they left it alone, Mike said,
and someone got hurt, then they'd be blempt for it.

I hold onto before, before our
tongues were twisted around corrected speech.

He was so grand he couldn't say Okay,
like the rest of us,
he said *Oh Kah*.

I ranted that we're educated into ignorance,
but can get jobs on the mainland
or at radio stations,
our voices do sound so homogeneous now.

But you watch it, my mother said,
it's your tongue too that was dipped
in the blue ink, and do go leaking iambics
all the day long.

The Tilts, Point Lance

Nights like this you could forget
you had a wife, kids, a town,
the sky so big, the ocean always there,
man alone to think about mortality.

Inside the smell of tobacco, dirty hair,
rubbed in cod guts, and diesel grease,
margarine, and burnt wool, stale rum sometimes,
grunts and nods enough, curses to punctuate.

Women want more, curtains, salt shakers,
nightcloths, verbs, wildflowers, french safes,
here it's stove, bunks, table, chairs.

A grin though going back on Saturday
always enough fish it's Cape St. Mary's
a grin in my lapel and make no mistake
glad to be back to civilization

one mile up the road.

Mike's

At first your daybed was a piece of board
nailed into the side of the wall
then your sister from the States saw one
in an antique shop in Delaware and
had it sent. You wouldn't lie on it

only sit, be afraid they'd think
I was Cleopatra, queen of the Nile
you said. It went to the store
leaned up against your flat.

In came the chesterfield with the bright
blue flowers and yellow background
now it has a dent in the middle
from your sharp hips and the one arm
worn down from your head resting
into the bowl of your hands.

In winter it is your nightbed too
with the old navy stock blanket
thrown over. You smell like my father
warm, old, musky. Woodsmoke grained
in your skin, stove oil soaked through your pores.

Your kitchen is your world, its once
white high-glossed walls now tinted amber
like the brun cafés in Amsterdam.
Chrome table, wood chairs, Holy Mary,
daybed, stove, cupboard, woodbox, telephone.

I doze sitting up, startle, you smile,
say, now you know why I need a bed there, girl.
I float in your kitchen, we talk little,
sweat a lot, gulp hot tea, and watch
the sun set into the sea.

Poem Without Beginning or End

because I can't see what's right before my
face, apparently: take how I barely noticed
the manner in which the faithful on their way
stopped beside that font, not only stopped
but how they dipped, and, after dipping, blessed:
what concerns me is their manner of blessing:

as gingerly is to reverently, as I extend
my fingers in this empty lunchtime lunchroom,
some dipped a hand inside as if to test
a hot iron, or the temperature of a bath,
then brought their glistening fingers up
to trace the line between forehead and chest,

then looped a stitch across the shoulders
left to right, or was it right to left —
I remember now, not having blessed myself
in years, I am certain — as it is a certainty
that repetition undermines certainty, try
signing one hundred traveller's cheques

one after another; after a while all you'll
remember is the simple motion (a motion
you spent long pre-verbal years in learning),
the follow-me-motion of the magician
that conjures in its wake, as in the wake
of that slow motion blessing, an aura,

a grey-blue length of typewriter ribbon,
an eye-spot drawn out into an egg-timer
with one end missing; a primitive petroglyph
of a primitive fish; an optician's doodle;
a bow tie glimpsed across a crowded room;
a serving table from the Bombay Company:

others, whether late or early, barely broke
their stride to dip, and, post-dipping, blessed
themselves offhandedly, as if dismissing
charity pleas or unsubstantiated claims,
as if shaking out a handkerchief, into which
there will be folded a commandeered wallet,

from which there will appear, transformed
(as I am changed by the magician's assistant —
my trousers make a tent when she bends over
to pick up the birdcage and there appears
on the tips of the magician's outstretched
fingers) a fluttering dove, or albino pigeon:

the slowness of that movement's sleight of
hand, the magic of that movement taking form,
I would see later, as second or third hand,
at the hands of one ageing Pablo Picasso:
the artist captured on stills from a film
sketching the studio air with a blowtorch,

the fiery bull appearing and disappearing
as the master beholds the camera with eyes
so bald and passionate they might have been
my father's looking down the dinner table,
but giving no clue as to whether this airing
was some new kind of art or a forgery:

The Crocus (after snow)

Look, where the lawn's pocket lolls —
there, a slim, disposable lighter
and another, their colours undiminished
purple and butterscotch yellow.

A flick of the wheel and sparks shoot out.
the flint is wet, but try again,
cup your hand around the little font —
there, stamens and pollen in that flare
and in its butane hum, the August bee.

I hear him, then he's gone.

And hard to take is the distance
he has to come. Hard as being wrong
about yourself and believing
that if you were wrong this once
it can never happen again.

The Heart

Many good angels helped me on my journey.

*

My mother watching from the garden gate,
her dress like liquid poured into a cup.

*

The butcher's voice: "Come down at three —
that's if your Mam will let you — come down
at three o'clock. I'll have one then."

*

Black cattle grazing the side of the hill,
their muzzy grazer's mouths, their lips that pluck
like fingers picking lint from table cloths.

*

The glitter-flip of wavelets on the lake
like a smashed up centre-piece decanter.

*

The gravel crunching underneath my boots.
The echo of my footsteps in the yard.

*

The lifting off of birds about the eaves.

*

Thoughts of Shep —
her prowling like a point of etiquette.

*

The hay shed's sudden buffeting swirl
that smells of stalk and yellow corn and hay,
the ripped-out circuitry of summer days.

*

The goose that waddles right across my path,
so near it almost bumps against my boots.
A telegram for Pat, I hear it say.

*

Coming back when I've been borne away
by smells of stalk and yellow corn and hay,
by thoughts of hay-barn lofts and loose chiffon.

*

Palms that screech along a wax-topped desk,
the sound that human skin would make caressed
if every pore contained a vocal chord.

*

The apparition of pigs within the piggery,
their little eyes so worldly wise and quick,
eyes that find in me some deficit.

*

The cat that bangs into a mirrored door
and shows me all I know of nonchalance.

*

The moment when I stop to check my watch;
a hard-shelled fly goes ping against my cheek.

*

That moment when the sunshine reappears
to set ablaze the holding pens ahead.

*

The sound of flies, their agitating wings
like Latin whispers from a congregation.

*

Black-faced sheep who wait with tongues stuck out
as children for a wafer of communion.

*

The butcher standing by the hoof-scarred door,
his shirt sleeves rolled,
his brow all slick with sweat.

*

The butcher dressed in rubber head to toe,
fresh from the field, the dragon slain, the quest
revealed as something other than expected.

*

The carcass skinned and steaming on the floor.
the deadbolt gun behind it on a hook.

*

The butcher reaching back around the door.
the heart as six-pack held in one flexed hand.

*

His fingers piping arteries and veins,
his head on tilt as if to catch a tune.

*

The heart above my open plastic bag — .
its queer inverted mountain shape,
its slender ox-blood tip and fatty snow
around the base — its sullen weight.

Summer Solstice

Call it the solstice, call it
the longest day of the year
for a fisherman's wife,
the longest day in the life
of his just-married daughter

There were few who
could fail to recall
the pure flood
of his crude, gifted tongue
at the table
There were those
who remembered
his last, careless dance;
though no one saw him
sway down a lane,
with a rose in his coat,
to the landwash

But his bow
slapped water
some time before daybreak;
and few would publicly say
why they thought his boat
threw him,
how or why
it was beached
at full throttle

When the sun had finally
called it a day
there were voices, lights
on the harbour;

and two quiet women
who watched in the dark
knew it would never be over

Longliner at Sunset

I'd watch her each evening
the little longliner
inching above my horizon
and as if the whole scene
were orchestrated by Newton
she and the sun
would meet
one rising, the other descending
precisely
at my horizon

I would see around her
a halo of saddlebacks
riding the sun
soon to be left to its fate
in her wake below
my horizon

Then after scudding the shafts
from streetlamps across the harbour
she'd dock
in the cigarette glow of men
who'd been told by the gulls
there was fish

Crocuses and Crown-of-Thorns

Through the winter's cold
it sucked the sun
heavy with sanguine blossoms
Spiked stem
and teardrop leaf
pressed into frosted pane:
a season's hoax, joyless
gaudy death

Saffron and violet crocuses
burst through snow this morning
Even before unfolding
they will know
a sparrow's exquisite breath
a starling's shadow

In 1951, PEI poet **Milton Acorn** (1923-1986) moved to Montreal, where, with his friend Al Purdy, he edited the literary magazine *Moment*. When Acorn's *I've Tasted My Blood* (1969) failed to win the Governor General's Award, poets Eli Mandel and Irving Layton organized a ceremony at Grossman's Tavern in Toronto and presented Acorn with the "People's Poet" medallion. In 1975 his *The Island Means Minago* won the Governor General's Award. Wherever he lived, Acorn's habit was to return to the Island once or twice a year, and he returned permanently in 1981.

Tammy Armstrong (1974), who grew up in St. Stephen, NB, has lived for eight years in Vancouver, where she earned an MFA from the University of British Columbia. Armstrong won the Writers' Federation of New Brunswick's Alfred G. Bailey Prize 2000. An excerpt from her first novel, *Translations: Aistreann* (2002), won the Writers' Federation of New Brunswick's David Adams Richards Prize in 1999.

Alfred G. Bailey (1905-1997) was born in Quebec City. He served as the first head of the University of New Brunswick History Department from 1938 to 1969. His literary interests led to the founding of the Bliss Carman Society in 1940 and to his co-founding of *The Fiddlehead*, Canada's oldest literary magazine, in 1945. From 1965 to 1969, he served as the university's Vice-President Academic. He published several scholarly historical and anthropological works, including *The Conflict of European and Eastern Algonkian Cultures* (1937; 1969). Bailey was made a Fellow of the Royal Society of Canada in 1951 and an officer of the Order of Canada in 1978.

A professor of literature and creative writing at St. Mary's University, **Brian Barlett** (1953) won the 2000 Petra Kenney Poetry Competition. In 1997 he won *The Malahat Review* Long Poem Prize for the second time. He was born and raised in New Brunswick, and as an undergraduate at the University of New Brunswick, he was part of the circle of writers who gathered at "Windsor Castle," Alden Nowlan's home. Bartlett is the editor of the forthcoming *Don MacKay: Essays on His Works* (2003).

Elizabeth Bishop (1911-1979) was born in Worcester, Massachusetts. Her father died shortly after her birth, and she spent her early childhood in Great Village, NS with her mother's extended family. After her mother's permanent hospitalization, she was taken back to the United States by her paternal grandparents. Throughout her life she made return trips to Nova Scotia and wrote extensively about the Maritimes in both her poetry and prose. Bishop's books won various prizes, including the Pulitzer Prize, the National Book Award, and the National Book Critics' Circle Award. Bishop was the consultant in poetry to the Library of Congress for 1949-50.

Poet and novelist **Lesley-Anne Bourne** (1964) was born in North Bay, Ontario. She is the recipient of the Milton Acorn Poetry Award, the Bliss Carman Poetry

Award, and the Carl Sentner Fiction Award. Bourne's debut novel, *The Bubble Star*, was published by Porcupine's Quill in 1998. She teaches Creative Writing at the University of Prince Edward Island.

Elizabeth Brewster (1922) was born in Chipman, NB. She has a PhD from the University of Indiana. Since 1972 she has been a member of the Department of English at the University of Saskatchewan, and is now Professor Emeritus. She was awarded the Saskatchewan Arts Board Lifetime Award for Excellence in the Arts (1995). Brewster was shortlisted for the Governor General's Award for Poetry in 1996 for *Footnotes to the Book of Job* (1995).

Charles Bruce (1906-1971) was born in Port Shoreham, NS. After gradu-ation from Mount Allison University in 1927, he joined the Canadian Press in Halifax, and was a member of the Song Fisherman, a group of regional poets that included Bliss Carman, Kenneth Leslie, and Charles G.D. Roberts. He worked as a war correspondent and in 1945 was appointed general super-intendent of the Canadian Press in Toronto. Bruce won the 1951 Governor General's Award for Poetry for *The Mulgrave Road*.

Born in Three Mile Plains, NS, **George Elliott Clarke** (1960) is a seventh-generation African Canadian. *Execution Poems* won the Governor General's Award in 2001. The opera *Beatrice Chancy* (1998) was produced in Toronto and Halifax. He has also written *Whylah Falls: The Play* (1999) and a feature film screenplay, *One Heart Broken Into Song* (1999). A professor of World Literature in English at the University of Toronto, Clarke is the editor of *Fire on the Water: An Anthology of Black Nova Scotian Writing* (1991-92) and *Eyeing the North Star: Directions in African-Canadian Literature* (1997). *Odysseys Home: Mapping African-Canadian Literature* was published by UTP In 2002. In 1998 he was the recipient of the Portia White Prize for Artistic Achievement.

Of both French and English ancestry, **Fred Cogswell** (1917) grew up on a farm in Carleton County, NB. He is widely known as a former editor of *The Fiddle-head* and publisher of Fiddlehead Poetry Books. He edited the two-volume *The Atlantic Anthology* (1985) and, with Jo-Anne Elder, translated and edited *Unfinished Dreams: Contemporary Poetry of Acadie* (1990). He is the editor and translator of *The Poetry of Modern Quebec* (1976). In 1995 he received the Alden Nowlan Award for Excellence in Literary Arts.

Geoffrey Cook (1963), born in Wolfville, NS, lives in Montreal and teaches Eng-lish at John Abbott College. He has published poems in numerous Canadian journals and is poetry editor for the on-line journal *The Danforth Review*.

Musician and poet **Allan Cooper** (1954) was born in Moncton, NB. From 1982 to 1991, he served as an editor of the literary journal *Germination*, and he is a publisher of Owl's Head Press. He was the first president of the Writers' Fede-ration of New Brunswick. His awards include the Alfred G. Bailey Prize in 1987 and 1992, and the Peter Gzowski Award in 1994.

Michael Crummey (1965) was born in Buchans, a mining town in central New-foundland. His novel *River Thieves*, nominated for the Giller Prize, won the Winterset Award, the Thomas Head Raddall Atlantic Fiction Prize and the

Atlantic Booksellers' Choice Award. He won the Bronwen Wallace Award for poetry.

Mary Dalton (1950) was born in Lake View, Conception Bay, NL. She was editor of *TickleAce* from 1980 to 1986. The author of two books of poetry, Dalton won the inaugural TickleAce Cabot Award for Poetry in 1998. She teaches in the Department of English at Memorial University.

Lynn Davies (1954) grew up in Moncton, NB, where her parents ran an independent bookstore, the Bookmark. After living for sixteen years in Nova Scotia, she moved to McLeod Hill, NB. Davies' first collection of poetry, *The Bridge That Carries the Road* (1999), was nominated for a Governor General's Award. Her children's stories have appeared in several anthologies.

Born in Long Pond, Conception Bay, NL, **Tom Dawe** (1940) is the author of sixteen books. After teaching at rural high schools, Dawe was appointed to the Department of English at Memorial University. He was a founding editor of Breakwater Books, the literary journal *TickleAce,* and the folklore journal *The Livyere.* A frequent winner of the Newfoundland and Labrador Arts and Letters Awards, Dawe was given a gold medal for visual arts in 1973.

Don Domanski (1950) was born on Cape Breton Island, NS. He has published seven books of poetry. Two of his recent books were shortlisted for the Governor General's Award, *Wolf-Ladder* (1991) and *Stations of the Left Hand* (1994). In 1999 he won the Canadian Literary Award for Poetry. Domanski currently lives and writes in Halifax, NS.

Robert Gibbs (1930) was born in Saint John, NB. He received a PhD from Cambridge and taught English at the University of New Brunswick from 1963 until his retirement in 1989. Gibbs has been both editor and poetry editor of *The Fiddlehead.* He has published two collections of short stories. His new manuscript of poetry is called *Driving to Our Edge.* He was co-editor *of Ninety Seasons: Modern Poets From The Maritimes* (1974).

Originally from Quebec, **Sue Goyette** (1964) lives in Cole Harbour, NS. Her first collection of poetry, *The True Names of Birds* (1999), was shortlisted for the Governor General's Award, the Gerald Lampert Memorial Award, and the Pat Lowther Memorial Award. Her debut novel is titled *Lures* (2002). She is at work on a new collection of poetry entitled *Undone.*

Richard Greene (1961) was born in St. John's, NL. In 1991 he received a PhD from the University of Oxford. He taught for some time at Memorial University and is currently an Assistant Professor of English at Erindale College, University of Toronto.

Elisabeth Harvor (1936), recipient of the Alden Nowlan Award for Excellence in Literary Arts (2000), grew up in the Kennebecasis Valley, NB. *Let Me Be the One* (1996), one of three collections of stories, was a finalist for the Governor General's Award for Fiction. Her first collection of poetry, *Fortress of Chairs* (1992), won the Gerald Lampert Memorial Award, and she has won First Prize in the League of Canadian Poets' National Poetry Competition and *The Malahat Review* Long Poem Prize. Harvor has published a novel, *Excessive Joy Injures the Heart* (2002).

David Helwig (1938) grew up in Ontario, and now lives in Belfast, PEI. Helwig is the author of sixteen works of fiction, most recently *The Time of Her Life* (2000) and *The Stand-In* (2002); numerous works of non-fiction; and twelve collections of poetry, including *This Human Day* (2000) and *Telling Stories* (2001).

Rita Joe (1931), a member of the Mi'kmaq First Nation, was born in Whyco-comagh, Cape Breton Island, NS. She has won several awards, including the Writers' Federation of Nova Scotia Prize and the National Aboriginal Achieve-ment Award. An officer of the Order of Canada, she has published four books of poetry and an autobiography, *Song of Rita Joe: Autobiography of a Mi'kmaq Poet* (1996).

M. Travis Lane (1934), a poet, reviewer, and critic, received her PhD from Cor-nell University. She has been a Graduate Research Associate for the Department of English at the University of New Brunswick since 1972. *Divinations and Shorter Poems 1973-1978* was awarded the Pat Lowther Memorial Award. *Keeping Afloat* (2001) won the 2002 Atlantic Poetry Prize.

Originally from New York City, writer and designer **Carole Langille** now lives in Lunenburg, NS. She has published two children's books and two collections of poetry. *In Cannon Cave* (1997) was shortlisted for the Governor General's Award and the Atlantic Poetry Prize. *Where the Wind Sleeps*, her second children's book, was a Canadian Children's Book Centre Choice for 1996.

Richard Lemm (1946) grew up in Seattle, Washington, came to Canada in 1967, and moved to Prince Edward Island in 1983. He is a professor of English and Creative Writing at the University of Prince Edward Island. From 1977 to 1987, he was a faculty member at the Banff School of Fine Arts, and he is a past president of the League of Canadian Poets. *Prelude to the Bacchanal* (1990) won the Canadian Authors' Association Award for poetry. Lemm was literary editor at Ragweed Press for three years, and he is the author of the biography *Milton Acorn: In Love and Anger* (1999).

Douglas Lochhead (1922) was born in Guelph, ON. In 1975 he was appointed Davidson Professor of Canadian Studies at Mount Allison University; he is now Professor Emeritus. He is a Senior Fellow and Founding Librarian at Massey College, University of Toronto. From 1989 to 1997 he was President of Goose Lane Editions. *High Marsh Road* was shortlisted for the 1980 Governor General's Award. *Weathers: Poems New & Selected* (2002) is his most recent collection.

Jeanette Lynes (1956) teaches English at St. Francis Xavier University. She is book review editor of *The Antigonish Review* and in 1999 she edited *Words Out There: Women Poets in Atlantic Canada*, an anthology of poems and interviews. She won the 2001 Bliss Carman Poetry Award.

Hugh MacDonald (1945), who lives in Montague, PEI, is a children's writer and co-editor of *Landmarks: An Anthology of New Atlantic Canadian Poetry of the Land* (2001). *Chung Lee Loves Lobsters* won the L.M. Montgomery Child-ren's Literature Award in 1990. He won the Atlantic Poetry Prize for *Looking for Mother* (1995).

John MacKenzie (1966) was born on Prince Edward Island. Having left school in grade seven, he worked in sawmills, bakeries, and kitchens, and on farms and construction crews. He lives in Charlottetown and is a co-founder of *blue SHIFT: A Journal of Poetry*. His first collection, *Sledgehammer and Other Poems* (2000), was shortlisted for the Atlantic Poetry Prize and the Gerald Lampert Memorial Award.

Brent MacLaine (1952), a fifth-generation Islander, grew up in Rice Point, PEI. He has taught at the University of Prince Edward Island since 1991. With Hugh MacDonald, he co-edited *Landmarks: An Anthology of New Atlantic Canadian Poetry of the Land* (2001). In 1992, he won the Milton Acorn Poetry Award. MacLaine's new manuscript is called *Where the Branch Bends*.

Poet laureate of Halifax, Sue MacLeod (1955) grew up in Ontario, the daughter of Cape Breton parents. Her first collection of poems, *The Language of Rain* (1995), was shortlisted for the Milton Acorn People's Poet Award. In 2000 she won *Arc* magazine's Poem of the Year Contest. She has two new manuscripts, *Mercy Bay* and *Five Readings of All This Snow*.

Randall Maggs (1944) was born in Vancouver, BC, and during his time in the Air Force lived in various regions of Canada. In 1977 he settled in Newfoundland, where he teaches at Sir Wilfred Grenfell College.

Carmelita McGrath (1960) was born in Branch, St. Mary's Bay, NL, and now makes her home in St. John's. In 1998 she received the Atlantic Poetry Prize for *To the New World*. Her collection of short stories, *Stranger Things Have Happened*, won the Writers' Alliance of Newfoundland and Labrador Bennington Gate Award.

Born and raised in Hamilton, Ontario, Robert Moore (1950) quit school at seventeen, though he later returned to complete a PhD at McMaster University. After teaching English and Drama at universities in Ontario and Alberta, he joined the faculty of the University of New Brunswick, Saint John. Moore is the author of a dozen plays, performed in various locations across the country.

Alden Nowlan (1933-1983) was born in Windsor, NS. Primarily self-educated, Nowlan worked as a newspaperman, and published poetry, plays, short stories, and novels. Writer-in-residence at the University of New Brunswick from 1969 to 1983, he was famous for the gatherings at his home, known as Windsor Castle. His awards include the Governor General's Award for Poetry in 1967 for *Bread, Wine and Salt* and a Guggenheim Fellowship (1967-68). *Alden Nowlan: Selected Poems* was published in 1996. The literary award for excellence for the province of New Brunswick is named in his honour. The annual Alden Nowlan Literary Festival in Fredericton honours his contribution to Canadian literature.

Prince Edward Islander Thomas O'Grady (1956) is Director of Irish Studies at the University of Massachusetts, Boston. He was educated at the University of Prince Edward Island, University College Dublin, and the University of Notre Dame.

Al Pittman (1940-2001), born in St. Leonard's, Placentia Bay, NL, was the author of numerous plays, stories, essays, and scripts for television and radio. He taught at Sir Wilfred Grenfell College in Corner Brook. He was inducted into the Newfoundland and Labrador Arts Council Hall of Honour. His last collection, *Thirty for Sixty* (1999), won the Writers' Alliance of Newfoundland and Labrador Book Award for Poetry.

matt robinson (1974), a native of Halifax, NS, now lives in Fredericton, NB. Winner of the 1999 Petra Kenney Poetry Competition and the 2001 Alfred G. Bailey Prize, he is a PhD student at the University of New Brunswick. His first collection of poetry, *A Ruckus of Awkward Stacking* (2000), was shortlisted for the Gerald Lampert Memorial Award and the ReLit Award for Poetry. He is on the editorial board of *The Fiddlehead*.

Gordon Rodgers (1952) was born in Gander, NL. He completed an MFA in Creative Writing at the University of British Columbia. He is currently a Registered Psychologist, practising on a part-time basis. His novel, *A Settlement of Memory* (1999), was shortlisted for the Writers' Alliance of Newfoundland and Labrador Bennington Gate Award.

Raised in Ontario, **Peter Sanger** (1943) was born in Worcestershire, England and was for twenty-six years a professor at the Nova Scotia Agricultural College in Truro. An editor of *The Antigonish Review*, Sanger also edited *John Thompson: Collected Poems and Translations* (1995). He founded the Elizabeth Bishop Society of Nova Scotia. His books on poetry include *SeaRun: Notes on John Thompson's "Stilt Jack"* (1986) and *"Her kindled shadow . . .": An Introduction to the Work of Richard Outram* (2001, 2002). A collection of essays, *Spar: Words in Place,* was published by Gapereau Press in 2002.

Born in Bridgewater, NS, and raised in Sydney, Cape Breton, **Joseph Sherman** (1945) received his MA in Creative Writing from the University of New Brunswick. He taught English at Centre Universitaire Saint-Louis-Maillet, Edmundston, NB, from 1970 to 1979, following which he was the editor of *ArtsAtlantic* in Charlottetown, PEI.

Anne Simpson (1956) lives in Antigonish, NS, where she teaches at the Writing Centre at St. Francis Xavier University. Her first collection of poetry, *Light Falls Through You* (2000), won the Atlantic Poetry Prize and the Gerald Lampert Memorial Award. Simpson's debut novel, *Canterbury Beach*, was a finalist for the Chapters/Robertson Davies Award in 1999.

Born in Ontario, raised in Newfoundland, **Sue Sinclair** (1972) lived for eight years in New Brunswick, where she studied at Mount Allison University and the University of New Brunswick. Sinclair was a finalist for the National Magazine Awards (1999) and the Chapters/Robertson Davies Award (1999). She is working on two poetry manuscripts, *Winter's Phantom Limb* and *Invisible in Daylight*.

Douglas Burnet Smith (1949) has served as President of the League of Canadian Poets and of the Public Lending Right Commission of Canada. He teaches at St. Francis Xavier University. Smith was nominated for the Governor General's Award for Poetry in 1993 for *Voices from a Farther Room* (1992) and for the Atlantic Poetry Prize for his most recent collection, *The Killed* (2000).

John Smith (1927) taught high school English in Toronto, and earned an MA in English at the University of Toronto. In 1967, he moved to Prince Edward Island, where he was a professor of English at the University of Prince Edward Island until his retirement in 1992. Smith's new manuscript is a collection of sonnets called *Fireflies in the Magnolia Grove*.

Kay Smith (1911) was born in Saint John, NB. A graduate in Drama from Columbia University, she taught English at Saint John Vocational High School. For three decades, she played a key role in the development of drama in Saint John. Associated with the Montreal poets of the 1950s, Smith's first collection, *Footnote to the Lord's Prayer* (1951), was published by First Statement Press and her selected poems, *The Bright Particulars*, was published by Ragweed in 1987.

Andrew Steeves (1970) was raised in Westmoreland County, NB, and he now lives in Wolfville, NS, where he completed an MA in English at Acadia University. Steeves is the co-publisher and editor of Gaspereau Press, and he was the editor of the *Gaspereau Review* through its complete run from 1997 to 2001.

John Steffler (1947) grew up near Thornhill, ON. In 1975, he began teaching at Sir Wilfred Grenfell College in Corner Brook, NL. His novel *The Afterlife of George Cartwright* won the Smithbooks/*Books in Canada* First Novel Award and was shortlisted for the Governor General's Award and the Commonwealth Prize for best first book in 1992. His other awards include the Thomas Head Raddall Atlantic Fiction Prize, the Newfoundland and Labrador Arts Council Artist of the Year Award, and the Atlantic Poetry Prize for his most recent collection, *That Night We Were Ravenous*.

Fraser Sutherland (1946), born in Pictou County, NS, now works as a writer and lexicographer in Toronto. He founded the literary journal *Northern Journey* in Montreal (1971-76). He has published eleven books, seven of which are collections of poetry.

Born in Manchester, England, **John Thompson** (1938-1976) moved to the United States in 1960. For his PhD thesis, Thompson translated the poetry of the French surrealist René Char. He moved to New Brunswick in 1966 to teach English at Mount Allison University. *Stilt Jack* (1978) consists of thirty-eight ghazals, and Thompson's working of the form has been a major influence on Canadian poetry. In 1991 Anansi Press published *I Dream Myself Into Being: Collected Poems*, and in 1995 Peter Sanger edited *John Thompson: Collected Poems & Translations*.

Michael Thorpe (1932) grew up in England and came to Canada in 1970 after teaching abroad for several years in Turkey, Nigeria, Singapore, and Holland. Thorpe taught at Mount Allison University where, until his retirement, he was Joseph Allison Professor of English. His critical work includes *Siegfried Sassoon: a Critical Study*; *The Poetry of Edmund Blunden*; and *Doris Lessing's Africa*.

Naturalist and nature writer **Harry Thurston** (1950) lives in Tidnish Bridge, NS, and travels widely to research articles for *Audubon*, *Canadian Geographic*, *Harrowsmith*, and *National Geographic*. He has been a contributing editor to *Equinox* since its inception in 1981. *Tidal Life: A Natural History of the Bay of*

Fundy earned him the Atlantic Booksellers' Choice Award, the City of Dartmouth Award, and the Evelyn Richardson Prize.

Eric Trethewey (1943) was born in Hants County, NS, and now lives in Roanoke, Virginia, where he teaches English at Hollins University. *Evening Knowledge* (1991) won second prize in the Virginia Prize for Poetry. Trethewey writes fiction and drama, and his screenplay *The Home Waltz* won the Virginia Governor's Screenwriting Competition in 1988.

Born in Saint John, NB, **R.M. Vaughan** (1965) now resides in Toronto. He holds a MA in Creative Writing from the University of New Brunswick. He is the author of a dozen plays, and he was the 1994-95 playwright-in-residence at Buddies in Bad Times. His first novel, *A Quilted Heart*, was published in 1998 by Insomniac.

Agnes Walsh (1950) was born and raised in Placentia, NL. She was a co-founder of Neighbourhood Dance Works and has been working in professional theatre for over twenty years. She divides her time between St. John's and Placentia Bay, where she is involved in community cultural development. Her research into the oral history of that area informs her poetry and drama.

Born in Claremorris, County Mayo, Ireland, **Patrick Warner** (1963) emigrated to Canada in 1980. He completed a Masters of Library and Information Science degree at the University of Western Ontario. He is the recipient of several Newfoundland and Labrador Arts and Letters Awards for poetry.

Enos Watts (1939), born in Long Pond, Conception Bay, NL, attended Memorial University, and taught in Stephenville. His work was included on Des Walsh's recording "10 Newfoundland Poets, Vol. 1" in 1985. He moved to St. John's after he retired from teaching.

Born in Luxembourg, **Liliane Welch** (1937) has lived for thirty-five years in Sackville, NB. A professor of French Studies at Mount Allison University, she is the co-author of *Emergence: Baudelaire, Mallarmé, Rimbaud* (1973) and *Address: Rimbaud Mallarmé Butor* (1979). Welch is also the author of two collections of essays, *Seismographs* (1988) and *Frescoes* (1998). She is the recipient of the Bressani Prize for *Life in Another Language* (1992) and the Writers' Federation of New Brunswick Alfred G. Bailey Prize (1986). In 1998 she was elected to the Institut Grand-Ducal, Luxembourg.

Alan R. Wilson was raised in Woodstock, NB, and now lives in British Columbia, where he is an analyst and statistician at the University of Victoria. *Before the Flood*, the first novel in a projected quartet, won the Chapters/ *Books in Canada* First Novel Award. A selection from his new manuscript of poems, *The Sonneteer's Sky Atlas*, a collection of eighty-eight sonnets, was a prizewinner in the CBC Literary Competition.

Acorn, Milton. *To Hear the Faint Bells*. Preface by James Deahl. Hamilton, ON: Hamilton Haiku Press, 1996.

_____. *Hundred Proof Earth*. Ed. James Deahl. Toronto, ON: Aya Press, 1988.

_____. *I Shout Love and Other Poems*. Ed. James Deahl. Toronto, ON: Aya Press, 1987.

_____. *The Uncollected Acorn*. Ed. James Deahl. Toronto, ON: Deneau Press, 1987.

_____ and James Deahl. *A Stand of Jackpine: Two Dozen Canadian Sonnets*. Toronto, ON: Unfinished Monument Press, 1987.

_____. *Whiskey Jack*. Toronto, ON: HMS, 1986.

_____. *Dig Up My Heart: Selected Poems 1952-83*. Toronto, ON: McClelland & Stewart, 1983, 1994.

_____. *Captain Neal MacDougal & the Naked Goddess: A Demi- Prophetic Work as a Sonnet-Series*. Charlottetown, PEI: Ragweed Press, 1982.

_____. *Jackpine Sonnets*. Toronto, ON: Steel Rail, 1977.

_____. *The Island Means Minago*. Toronto, ON: NC Press, 1975.

_____. *More Poems for People*. Toronto, ON: NC Press, 1972.

_____. *I've Tasted My Blood: Poems 1956 to 1968*. Toronto, ON: Ryerson Press, 1969.

_____. *Jawbreakers*. Toronto, ON: Contact Press, 1963.

_____. *The Brain's the Target*. Toronto, ON: Ryerson Press, 1960.

_____. *Against a League of Liars*. Toronto, ON: Hawkshead Press, 1960.

_____. *In Love and Anger*. Montreal, QC: self-published, 1956.

Armstrong, Tammy. *Bogman's Music*. Vancouver, BC: Anvil Press, 2001.

Bailey, Alfred G.. *The Sun, the Wind, the Summer Field*. Fredericton, NB: Goose Lane Editions, 1996.

_____. *Miramichi Lightning*. Fredericton, NB: Fiddlehead Poetry Books, 1981.

_____. *Thanks for a Drowned Island*. Toronto, ON: McClelland & Stewart, 1973.

_____. *Border River*. Toronto, ON: McClelland & Stewart, 1952.

_____. *Tao*. Toronto, ON: Ryerson Chapbooks, 1930.

_____. *Songs of the Saguenay & Other Poems*. Quebec, QC: Chronicle Telegraph Publishing, 1927.

Bartlett, Brian. *The Afterlife of Trees*. Montreal, QC: McGill-Queen's University Press, 2002.

_____. *Granite Erratics*. Victoria, BC: Ekstasis Editions, 1997.

_____. *Underwater Carpentry*. Fredericton, NB: Goose Lane Editions, 1993.

_____. *Planet Harbour*. Fredericton, NB: Goose Lane Editions, 1989.

_____. *Cattail Week*. Montreal, QC: Villeneuve, 1981.

_____. *Brother's Insomnia*. Fredericton, NB: New Brunswick Chapbooks, 1972.

_____. *Finches for the Wake*. Fredericton, NB: Fiddlehead Poetry Books, 1971.

Bishop, Elizabeth. *The Complete Poems 1927-1979*. New York, NY: Farrar, Straus & Giroux, 1979.

_____. *Geography III*. New York, NY: Farrar, Straus & Giroux, 1976.

_____. *Questions of Travel*. New York, NY: Farrar, Straus & Giroux, 1965.

_____. *A Cold Spring*. Boston, MA: Houghton Mifflin, 1955.

_____. *North & South*. Boston, MA: Houghton Mifflin, 1946.

Bourne, Lesley-Anne. *Field Day*. Waterloo, ON: Penumbra Press, 1996.

_____. *Skinny Girls*. Waterloo, ON: Penumbra Press, 1993.

_____. *The Story of Pears*. Waterloo, ON: Penumbra Press, 1990.

Brewster, Elizabeth. *Burning Bush*. Ottawa, ON: Oberon, 2000.

_____. *Garden of Sculpture*. Ottawa, ON: Oberon, 1998.

_____. *Footnotes to the Book of Job*. Ottawa, ON: Oberon, 1995.

_____. *Wheel of Change*. Ottawa, ON: Oberon, 1993.

_____. *Spring Again: Poems*. Ottawa, ON: Oberon, 1990.

_____. *Entertaining Angels*. Ottawa, ON: Oberon, 1988.

_____. *Selected Poems of Elizabeth Brewster*. 2 vols. Ottawa, ON: Oberon, 1985.

_____. *Digging In: New Poems*. Ottawa, ON: Oberon, 1982.

_____. *The Way Home: New Poems*. Ottawa, ON: Oberon, 1982.

_____. *Poems*. Ottawa, ON: Oberon, 1977.

_____. *In Search of Eros*. Toronto, ON: Clarke Irwin, 1974.

_____. *Sunrise North*. Toronto, ON: Clarke Irwin, 1972.

_____. *Passage of Summer*. Toronto, ON: Ryerson Press, 1969.

_____. *Roads and Other Poems*. Toronto, ON: Ryerson Press, 1957.

_____. *Lillooet*. Toronto, ON: Ryerson Press, 1954.

Bruce, Charles. *The Mulgrave Road: Selected Poems of Charles Bruce*. Ed. Andy Wainwright and Lesley Choyce. Porters Lake, NS: Pottersfield Press, 1985.

_____. *The Mulgrave Road*. Toronto, ON: Macmillan, 1951.

_____. *The Flowing Summer*. Toronto, ON: Ryerson Press, 1947.

_____. *Grey Ship Moving*. Toronto, ON: Ryerson Press, 1945.

_____. *Tomorrow's Tide*. Toronto, ON: Macmillan, 1932.

_____. *Wild Apples*. Sackville, NB: privately published, 1927.

Clarke, George Elliott. *Black*. Vancouver, BC: Polestar, forthcoming, 2003.

_____. *Blue*. Vancouver, BC: Polestar, 2001.

_____. *Blue (II)*. Montreal, QC: Cumulus Press, 2001.

_____. *Execution Poems*. Wolfville, NS: Gaspereau Press, 2001.

_____. *Gold Indigoes*. Durham, NC: Carolina Wren Press, 2000.

_____. *Beatrice Chancy*. Vancouver, BC: Polestar, 1999.

_____. *Provençal Songs II*. Ottawa, ON: above/ground press, 1997.

_____. *Lush Dreams, Blue Exile: Fugitive Poems 1978-1993*. Porters Lake, NS: Pottersfield Press, 1994.

_____. *Provençal Songs*. [Ottawa, ON]: Magnum Book Store, 1993.

_____. *Whylah Falls*. Vancouver, BC: Polestar Book Publishers, 1990. 2nd Ed. 2000.

_____. *Saltwater Spirituals and Deeper Blues*. Porters Lake, NS: Pottersfield Press, 1983.

Cogswell, Fred. *Dried Flowers*. Ottawa, ON: Borealis Press, 2002.

_____. *Deeper Than Mind*. Ottawa, ON: Borealis Press, 2001.

_____. *With Vision Added*. Nepean, ON: Borealis Press, 2000.

_____. *A Double Question*. Nepean, ON: Borealis Press, 1999.

_____. *Folds*. Nepean, ON: Borealis Press, 1997.

_____. *The Trouble with Light*. Ottawa, ON: Borealis Press, 1996.

_____. *As I See It*. Ottawa, ON: Borealis Press, 1994.

_____. *In My Own Growing*. Ottawa, ON: Borealis Press, 1993.

_____. _In Praise of Old Music_. Ottawa, ON: Borealis Press, 1992.

_____. _When the Right Light Shines_. Ottawa, ON: Borealis Press, 1992.

_____. _Watching an Eagle_. Ottawa, ON: Borealis Press, 1991.

_____. _Black and White Tapestry_. Ottawa, ON: Borealis Press, 1989.

_____. _The Best Notes Merge_. Ottawa, ON: Borealis Press, 1988.

_____. _Meditations: 50 Sestinas_. Charlottetown, PEI: Ragweed Press, 1986.

_____. _Pearls_. Charlottetown, PEI: Ragweed Press, 1983.

_____. _Selected Poems_. Montreal, QC: Guernica Editions, 1983.

_____. _A Long Apprenticeship: Collected Poems_. Fredericton, NB: Fiddlehead Poetry Books, 1980.

_____. _Against Perspective_. Fredericton, NB: Fiddlehead Poetry Books, 1977.

_____. _Light Bird of Life: Selected Poems_. Fredericton, NB: Fiddlehead Poetry Books, 1974.

_____. _The House Without a Door_. Fredericton, NB: Fiddlehead Poetry Books, 1973.

_____. _The Chains of Liliput_. Fredericton, NB: Fiddlehead Poetry Books, 1971.

_____. _In Praise of Chastity_. Fredericton, NB: University of New Brunswick, 1970.

_____. _Immortal Plowman_. Fredericton, NB: Fiddlehead Poetry Books, 1969.

_____. _Star-People_. Fredericton, NB: Fiddlehead Poetry Books, 1968.

_____. _Lost Dimension_. Dulwich Village, UK: Outposts Publications, 1960.

_____. _Descent from Eden_. Toronto, ON: Ryerson Press, 1959.

_____. _The Haloed Tree_. Toronto, ON: Ryerson Press, 1956.

_____. _The Stunted Strong_. Fredericton, NB: University of New Brunswick, 1954.

Cook, Geoffrey. _Postscript_. Montreal, QC: Signal Editions, forthcoming 2004.

Cooper, Allan. _Singing the Flowers Open_. Wolfville, NS: Gaspereau Press, 2001.

_____. _Heaven of Small Moments_. Fredericton, NB: Broken Jaw Press, 1998.

_____. _The Deer Is Thirsty for the Mountain Stream_. Alma, NB: Owl's Head Press, 1992.

_____. _The Pearl Inside the Body: New and Selected Poems_. Sackville, NB: Percheron Press, 1991.

_____. _To an Unborn Child_. Fort Collins, CO: Leaping Mountains Press, 1988.

_____. _Poems Released on a Nuclear Wind_. Porters Lake, NS: Pottersfield Press, 1987.

_____. _Jottings Toward the Country of Light: 10 Ghazals_. Brandon, MB: Pierian Press, 1984.

_____. _Bending the Branch_. Sackville, NB: Percheron Press, 1983.

_____. _Hidden River Poems_. Fredericton, NB: Fiddlehead Poetry Books, 1982.

_____. _Blood-Lines_. Fredericton, NB: Fiddlehead Poetry Books, 1979.

Crummey, Michael. _Salvage_. Toronto, ON: McClelland & Stewart, 2002.

_____. _Emergency Roadside Assistance_. Stratford, ON: Trout Lily Press, 2001.

_____. _Hard Light_. London, ON: Brick Books, 1998.

_____. _Arguments with Gravity_. Kingston, ON: Quarry Press, 1996.

Dalton, Mary. _Merrybegot_. St. John's, NL: Running the Goat, 2002.

_____. _Allowing the Light: Poems_. St. John's, NL: Breakwater Books, 1993.

_____. _The Time of Icicles: Poems_. St. John's, NL: Breakwater Books, 1989.

Davies, Lynn. _The Bridge That Carries the Road_. London, ON: Brick Books, 1999.

Dawe, Tom. _In Hardy Country: New and Selected Poems_. St. John's, NL: Breakwater Books, 1993.

_____. _A Gommil from Bumble Bee Bight and Other Nonsense Verse_. St. John's, NL: Harry Cuff Publications, 1982.

———. *Island Spell*. St. John's, NL: Harry Cuff Publications, 1981.

———. *In a Small Cove*. Chipping Norton, UK: Wychwood Press, 1978.

———. *Hemlock Cove and After*. Portugal Cove, NL: Breakwater Books, 1975.

———. *Connections: Poems*. St. John's, NL: Memorial University of Newfoundland, 1972.

Domanski, Don. *Parish of the Physic Moon*. Toronto, ON: McClelland & Stewart, 1998.

———. *Stations of the Left Hand*. Toronto, ON: Coach House Press, 1994.

———. *Wolf-Ladder*. Toronto, ON: Coach House Press, 1991.

———. *Hammerstroke*. Toronto, ON: House of Anansi Press, 1986.

———. *War in an Empty House*. Toronto, ON: House of Anansi Press, 1982.

———. *Heaven*. Toronto, ON: House of Anansi Press, 1978.

———. *The Cape Breton Book of the Dead*. Toronto, ON: House of Anansi Press, 1975.

Gibbs, Robert. *Earth Aches*. Fredericton, NB: Wild East (Salamanca Chapbook Series), 1991; rpt. Fredericton, NB: Broken Jaw, 1995.

———. *The Tongue Still Dances: Poems New and Selected*. Fredericton, NB: Fiddlehead PoetryBooks & Goose Lane Editions, 1985.

———. *All This Night Long*. Fredericton, NB: Fiddlehead Poetry Books, 1978.

———. *A Kind of Wakefulness*. Fredericton, NB: Fiddlehead Poetry Books, 1973.

———. *A Dog in a Dream*. Fredericton, NB: New Brunswick Chapbooks, 1971.

———. *Earth Charms Heard So Early*. Fredericton, NB: Fiddlehead Poetry Books, 1970.

———. *The Road from Here*. Fredericton, NB: New Brunswick Chapbooks, 1968.

Goyette, Susan. *The True Names of Birds*. London, ON: Brick Books, 1998.

Greene, Richard. *Republic of Solitude: Poems 1984-1994*. St. John's, NL: Breakwater Books, 1994.

Harvor, Elisabeth. *The Long Cold Green Evenings of Spring*. Montreal, QC: Signal Editions, 1997.

———. *Fortress of Chairs*. Montreal, QC: Signal Editions, 1992.

Helwig, David. *Telling Stories*. Ottawa, ON: Oberon Press, 2001.

———. *This Human Day*. Ottawa, ON: Oberon Press, 2000.

———. *A Random Gospel*. Ottawa, ON: Oberon Press, 1996.

———. *The Beloved*. Ottawa, ON: Oberon Press, 1992.

———. *The Hundred Old Names*. Ottawa, ON: Oberon Press, 1989.

———. *Catchpenny Poems*. Ottawa, ON: Oberon Press, 1983.

———. *The Rain Falls Like Rain*. Ottawa, ON: Oberon Press, 1982.

———. *A Book of the Hours*. Ottawa, ON: Oberon Press, 1979.

———. *Atlantic Crossings*. Ottawa, ON: Oberon Press, 1974.

———. *The Best Name of Silence*. Ottawa, ON: Oberon Press, 1972.

———. *The Sign of the Gunman*. Ottawa, ON: Oberon Press, 1969.

———. *Figures in a Landscape*. Ottawa, ON: Oberon Press, 1968.

Joe, Rita. *We Are The Dreamers: Recent and Early Poetry*. Wreck Cove, NS: Breton Books, 1999.

———. *Lnu and Indians We're Called*. Charlottetown, PEI: Ragweed Press, 1991.

———. *Song of Eskasoni: More Poems of Rita Joe*. Charlottetown, PEI: Ragweed Press, 1988.

———. *Poems of Rita Joe*. Halifax, NS: Abanaki Press, 1978.

Lane, M. Travis. *Keeping Afloat*. Montreal, QC: Guernica Editions, 2001.

———. *Night Physics*. London, ON: Brick Books, 1994.

———. *Temporary Shelter: Poems 1986-1990*. Fredericton, NB: Goose Lane Editions, 1993.

———. *Solid Things: Poems New and Selected*. Dunvegan, ON: Cormorant Books, 1989.

———. *Reckonings*. Fredericton, NB: Fiddlehead Poetry Books & Goose Lane Editions, 1988.

———. *Divinations and Shorter Poems 1973-1978*. Fredericton, NB: Fiddlehead Poetry Books & Goose Lane Editions, 1980.

———. *Homecomings*. Fredericton, NB: Fiddlehead Poetry Books, 1977.

———. *Poems 1968-1972*. Fredericton, NB: Fiddlehead Poetry Books, 1973.

———. *An Inch or So of Garden*. Fredericton, NB: New Brunswick Chapbooks, 1969.

Langille, Carole Glasser. *Late in a Slow Time* Toronto, ON: Mansfield Press, forthcoming, 2003.

———. *In Cannon Cave*. London, ON: Brick Books, 1997.

———. *All That Glitters in Water: Poetry*. Baltimore, MD: New Poets Series, 1990.

Lemm, Richard. *Four Ways of Dealing with Bullies*. Toronto, ON: Wolsak and Wynn, 2000.

———. *Prelude to the Bacchanal*. Charlottetown, PEI: Ragweed Press, 1990.

———. *A Difficult Faith*. Porters Lake, NS: Pottersfield Press, 1985.

———. *Dancing in Asylum*. Porters Lake, NS: Pottersfield Press, 1982.

Lochhead, Douglas. *Weathers: Poems New and Selected*. Fredericton, NB: Goose Lane Editions, 2002.

———. *Yes, Yes, Yes!*. Wolfville, NS: Gaspereau Press, 2001.

———. *Cape Enragé: Poems on a Raised Beach*. Toronto, ON: Wolsak and Wynn, 2000.

———. *The Lucretius Poems*. Sackville, NB: Harrier Editions, 1998.

———. *All Things Do Continue: Poems of Celebration*. Toronto, ON: St. Thomas Poetry Series, 1997.

———. *Breakfast at Mel's and Other Poems of Love and Places*. Fredericton, NB: Goose Lane Editions, 1997.

———. *Charlie, Boo Boo, Nutley Clutch & Others: Twelve Canadian Jollies, Lovelies*. Sackville, NB: Harrier Editions, 1997.

———. *Homage to Henry Alline & Other Poems*. Fredericton, NB: Goose Lane Editions, 1992.

———. *Black Festival: A Long Poem*. Sackville, NB: Harrier Editions, 1991.

———. *Dykelands*. Montreal, QC: McGill-Queen's University Press, 1989.

———. *Upper Cape Poems*. Fredericton, NB: Goose Lane Editions, 1989.

———. *Tiger in the Skull: New and Selected Poems. 1959-1985*. Fredericton, NB: Fiddlehead Poetry Books & Goose Lane Editions, 1986.

———. *The Panic Field*. Fredericton, NB: Fiddlehead Poetry Books & Goose Lane Editions, 1984.

———. *A&E*. Sackville, NB: Harrier Editions, 1980.

———. *Battle Sequence*. Sackville, NB: Harrier Editions, 1980.

———. *High Marsh Road: Lines for a Diary*. Toronto, ON: Anson-Cartwright Editions, 1980. Fredericton, NB: Goose Lane Editions, 1996.

———. *The Full Furnace: Collected Poems*. Toronto, ON: McGraw-Hill Ryerson, 1975.

———. *Prayers in a Field*. Toronto, ON: Aliquando Press, 1974.

_____. *Millwood Road Poems*. Toronto, ON: Roger Ascham Press, 1970.

_____. *A&B&C&: An Alphabet*. Toronto, ON: Three Fathom Press, 1969.

_____. *It Is All Around*. Toronto, ON: Ryerson Press, 1960.

_____. *The Heart Is Fire*. Toronto, ON: Ryerson Press, 1959.

Lynes, Jeanette. [Untitled]. Toronto, ON: Wolsak and Wynn, forthcoming, 2003.

_____. *A Woman Alone on the Atikokan Highway*. Toronto, ON: Wolsak and Wynn, 1999.

MacDonald, Hugh. *Tossed Like Weeds from the Garden*. Windsor, ON: Black Moss Press, 1999.

_____. *The Digging of Deep Wells*. Windsor, ON: Black Moss Press, 1997.

_____. *Looking for Mother*. Windsor, ON: Black Moss Press, 1995.

MacKenzie, John. *Shaken by Physics*. Vancouver, BC: Polestar, 2002.

_____. *Sledgehammer and Other Poems*. Vancouver, BC: Polestar, 2000.

MacLaine, Brent. *Wind & Root*. Montreal, QC: Signal Editions, 2000.

MacLeod, Sue. *The Language of Rain*. Lockeport, NS: Roseway, 1995.

Maggs, Randall. *Timely Departures*. St. John's, NL: Breakwater Books, 1994.

McGrath, Carmelita. *Ghost Poems*. St. John's, NL: Running the Goat, 2001.

_____. *To the New World*. St. John's, NL: Killick Press, 1997.

_____. *Poems on Land and on Water*. St. John's, NL: Killick Press, 1992.

Moore, Robert. *So Rarely in Our Skins*. Winnipeg, MB: The Muses' Company, 2002.

Nowlan, Alden. *Selected Poems*. Eds. Patrick Lane and Lorna Crozier. Concord, ON: House of Anansi Press, 1996.

_____. *The Best of Alden Nowlan*. Ed. Allison Mitcham. Hantsport, NS: Lancelot Press, 1993.

_____. *What Happened When He Went to the Store for Bread*. Saint Paul, MN: Nineties Press, 1993.

_____. *An Exchange of Gifts: Poems New and Selected*. Ed. Robert Gibbs. Toronto, ON: Irwin,1985.

_____. *Early Poems*. Fredericton, NB: Fiddlehead Poetry Books, 1983.

_____. *I Might Not Tell Everybody This*. Toronto, ON: Clarke Irwin, 1982.

_____. *The Gardens of the Wind*. Saskatoon, SK: Thistledown Press, 1982.

_____. *Smoked Glass*. Toronto, ON: Clarke Irwin, 1977.

_____. *I'm a Stranger Here Myself*. Toronto, ON: Clarke Irwin, 1974.

_____ and Tom Forrestall. *Shaped by This Land*. Fredericton, NB: Brunswick Press, 1974.

_____. *Between Tears and Laughter*. Toronto, ON: Clarke Irwin, 1971.

_____. *Playing the Jesus Game*. Intro. Robert Bly. Trumansburg, NY: New/Books, 1970. rpt. Trumansburg, NY: Crossing Press, 1973.

_____. *The Mysterious Naked Man*. Toronto, ON: Clarke Irwin, 1969.

_____. *A Black Plastic Button and a Yellow Yoyo: Poems*. Toronto, ON: C. Pachter, 1968.

_____. *Bread, Wine and Salt*. Toronto, ON: Clarke Irwin, 1967.

_____. *The Things Which Are*. Toronto, ON: Contact Press, 1962.

_____. *Under the Ice*. Toronto, ON: Ryerson Press, 1961.

_____. *Wind in a Rocky Country*. Toronto, ON: An Emblem Book, 1960.

_____. *A Darkness in the Earth*. Eureka, CA: Hearse Press, 1959.

_____. *The Rose and the Puritan*. Fredericton, NB: University of New Brunswick, 1958.

O'Grady, Thomas. *What Really Matters*. Montreal, QC: McGill-Queen's University Press, 2000.

Pittman, Al. *Thirty-for-Sixty*. St. John's, NL: Breakwater Books, 1999.

_____. *Dancing in Limbo: Poems*. St. John's, NL: Breakwater Books, 1993.

_____. *On a Wing and a Wish: Salt Water Bird Rhymes*. St. John's, NL: Breakwater Books, 1992.

_____. *Once when I was drowning: poems*. St. John's, NL: Breakwater Books, 1978.

_____. *Through One More Window*. Portugal Cove, NL: Breakwater Books, 1974.

_____. *Seaweed and Rosaries*. Montreal, QC: Poverty Press, 1969.

_____. *The Elusive Resurrection*. Fredericton, NB: Brunswick Press, 1966.

robinson, matt. *How We Play at It: A List*. Toronto, ON: ECW, 2002.

_____. *A Ruckus of Awkward Stacking*. Toronto, ON: Insomniac, 2001.

Rodgers, Gordon. *The Pyrate Latitudes: Poems*. St. John's, NL: Creative Publishers, 1986.

_____. *Floating Houses: Poems*. St. John's, NL: Creative Publishers, 1984.

Sanger, Peter. *Kerf*. Wolfville, NS: Gaspereau Press, 2002.

_____ and Thaddeus Holownia. *Ironworks*. Jolicure, NB: Anchorage Editions, 2001.

_____. *After Monteverde: Twelve Poems*. Sackville, NB: Harrier Editions, 1997.

_____. *The Third Hand*. Jolicure, NB: Anchorage Press, 1994.

_____. *Earth Moth*. Fredericton, NB: Goose Lane Editions, 1991.

_____. *The America Reel*. Porters Lake, NS: Pottersfield Press, 1983.

Sherman, Joseph. *American Standard and Other Poems*. Ottawa, ON: Oberon Press, 2001.

_____. *Shaping the Flame: Imagining Wallenberg*. Ottawa, ON: Oberon Press, 1989.

_____. *Lords of Shouting*. Ottawa, ON: Oberon Press, 1982.

_____. *Chaim the Slaughterer*. Ottawa, ON: Oberon Press, 1974.

_____. *Birthday*. Fredericton, NB: New Brunswick Chapbook, 1969.

Simpson, Anne. *Timepiece*. Toronto, ON: McClelland & Stewart, 2002.

_____. *Light Falls Through You*. Toronto, ON: McClelland & Stewart, 2000.

Sinclair, Sue. *Secrets of Weather & Hope*. London, ON: Brick Books, 2001.

Smith, Douglas Burnet. *Helsinki Drift: Travel Poems*. Vancouver, BC: Beach Holme Publishing, 2002.

_____. *Chainletter*. Stratford, ON: Trout Lily Press, 2001.

_____. *The Killed*. Toronto, ON: Wolsak and Wynn, 2000.

_____. *Two Minutes for Holding*. Concord, ON: House of Anansi Press, 1995.

_____. *Voices from a Farther Room*. Don Mills, ON: Wolsak and Wynn, 1992.

_____. *The Knife-Thrower's Partner*. Toronto, ON: Wolsak and Wynn, 1989.

_____. *Ladder to the Moon*. Ilderton, ON: Brick Books/Coldstream, 1988.

_____. *Living in the Cave of the Mouth*. Riverview, NB: Owl's Head Press, 1986.

_____. *Scarecrow*. Winnipeg, MB: Turnstone Press, 1980.

_____. *The Light of Our Bones*. Winnipeg, MB: Turnstone Press, 1980.

_____. *Thaw*. Winnipeg, MB: Four Humours Press, 1977.

Smith, John. *Strands the Length of the Wind*. Charlottetown, PEI: Ragweed Press, 1993.

_____. *Midnight Found You Dancing*. Charlottetown, PEI: Ragweed Press, 1986.

_____. *Sucking-Stones*. Dunvegan, ON: Quadrant Editions, 1982.

_____. *Of the Swimmer Among the Coral and of the Monk in the Mountains.* Charlottetown, PEI: Square Deal Publications, 1976.

_____. *Winter in Paradise.* Charlottetown, PEI: Square Deal Publications, 1972.

Smith, Kay. *The Bright Particulars: Poems Selected and New.* Charlottetown, PEI: Ragweed Press, 1987.

_____. *When a Girl Looks Down.* Fredericton, NB: Fiddlehead Poetry Books, 1978.

_____. *At the Bottom of the Dark.* Fredericton, NB: Fiddlehead Poetry Books, 1971.

_____. *Footnote to the Lord's Prayer and Other Poems.* Montreal, QC: First Statement Press, 1951.

Steeves, Andrew. *Improbable Cures.* Wolfville. NS: privately printed, 2000.

_____. *Stone Fire Water.* Wolfville, NS: privately printed, 1999.

_____. *Cutting the Devil's Throat.* Fredericton, NB: Goose Lane Editions, 1998.

Steffler, John. *Helix: New and Selected Poems.* Montreal, QC: Signal Editions, 2002.

_____. *That Night We Were Ravenous.* Toronto, ON: McClelland & Stewart, 1998.

_____. *The Wreckage of Play.* Toronto, ON: McClelland & Stewart, 1988.

_____. *The Grey Islands: A Journey.* Toronto, ON: McClelland & Stewart, 1985. Reprinted as *The Grey Islands.* London, ON: Brick Books, 2000.

_____. *An Explanation of Yellow.* Ottawa, ON: Borealis Press, 1980.

Sutherland, Fraser, and Goran Simic. *Peace and War.* Toronto, ON: Coach House Press, 1998.

Sutherland, Fraser. *Jonestown: A Poem.* Toronto, ON: McClelland & Stewart, 1996.

_____. *Whitefaces.* Windsor, ON: Black Moss Press, 1986.

_____. *Madwomen: Poems.* Windsor, ON: Black Moss Press, 1978.

_____. *Within the Wound: Remembering H.D.S.* Ottawa, ON: Northern Journey Press, 1976.

_____. *In the Wake of.* Ottawa, ON: Northern Journey Press, 1974.

_____. *Strange Ironies.* Fredericton, NB: Fiddlehead Poetry Books, 1972.

Thompson, John. *Collected Poems & Translations.* Ed. Peter Sanger. Fredericton, NB: Goose Lane Editions, 1995.

_____. *I Dream Myself into Being: Collected Poems.* Intro. James Polk. Toronto, ON: House of Anansi Press, 1991.

_____. *Stilt Jack.* Toronto, ON: House of Anansi Press, 1978.

_____. *At the Edge of the Chopping There Are No Secrets.* Toronto, ON: House of Anansi Press, 1973.

Thorpe, Michael. *The Unpleasant Subject: Sketches Around Hitler.* Toronto, ON: TSAR, 2001.

_____. *Loves and Other Poems.* Toronto, ON: TSAR, 1997.

_____. *Animal Relations.* Fredericton, NB: Wild East (Salamanca Chapbooks Series), 1991.

_____. *Bagdad is Everywhere: Poems 1984-1991.* Toronto, ON: TSAR, 1991.

_____. *The Observing Eye.* London, ON: Third Eye Publications, 1988.

_____. *Out of the Storm.* Moonbeam, ON: Penumbra Press, 1984.

_____. *By the Niger and Other Poems.* London, England: Fortune Press, 1969.

Thurston, Harry. *If Men Lived on Earth.* Wolfville, NS: Gaspereau Press, 2000.

_____. *Clouds Flying Before the Eye.* Fredericton, NB: Fiddlehead Poetry Books & Goose Lane Editions, 1985.

_____. *Barefaced Stone.* Fredericton, NB: Fiddlehead Poetry Books, 1980.

Trethewey, Eric. *The Long Road Home*. Fredericton, NB: Goose Lane Editions, 1994.

———. *Evening Knowledge*. Cleveland, OH: Cleveland State University Poetry Center, 1991.

———. *Dreaming of Rivers*. Cleveland, OH: Cleveland State University Poetry Center, 1984.

Vaughan, R.M. *Invisible to Predators*. Toronto, ON: ECW Press, 1999.

———. *96 tears (In My Jeans)*. Fredericton, NB: Broken Jaw Press, 1997.

———. *A Selection of Dazzling Scarves*. Toronto, ON: ECW Press, 1996.

———. *The InCorrupt Tables*. Fredericton, NB: Wild East, 1992; rpt. Fredericton, NB: Broken Jaw, 1995.

Walsh, Agnes. *In the Old Country of My Heart*. St. John's, NL: Killick Press, 1996.

Warner, Patrick. *All Manner of Misunderstanding*. St. John's, NL: Killick Press, 2001.

Watts, Enos. *Autumn Vengeance*. St. John's, NL: Breakwater Books, 1986.

———. *After the Locusts*. Portugal Cove, NL: Breakwater Books, 1974.

Welch, Liliane. *Untethered in Paradise*. Ottawa, ON: Borealis Press, 2002.

———. *Unlearning Ice*. Ottawa, ON: Borealis Press, 2001.

———. *The Rock's Stillness*. Ottawa, ON: Borealis Press, 1999.

———. *Mosaics: Music Scapes Words*. Luxembourg: Imprimerie Centrale, 1998.

———. *Fidelities*. Ottawa, ON: Borealis Press, 1997.

———. *Dream Museum*. Victoria, BC: Sono Nis Press, 1995.

———. *Von Menschen und Orten*. Luxembourg: Les Cahiers Luxemburgeois, 1992.

———. *Life in Another Language*. Dunvegan, ON: Cormorant Books, 1992.

———. *Fire to the Looms Below*. Charlottetown, PEI: Ragweed Press, 1990.

———. *Word-House of a Grandchild*. Charlottetown, PEI: Ragweed Press, 1987.

———. *Manstorna: Life on the Mountain*. Charlottetown, PEI: Ragweed Press, 1985.

———. *Unrest Bound*. Brandon, MB: Pierian Press, 1985.

———. *From the Songs of the Artisans*. Fredericton, NB: Fiddlehead Poetry Books, 1983.

———. *Brush and Trunks*. Fredericton, NB: Fiddlehead Poetry Books, 1981.

———. *October Winds*. Fredericton, NB: Fiddlehead Poetry Books, 1980.

———. *Assailing Beats*. Ottawa, ON: Borealis Press, 1979.

———. *Syntax of Ferment*. Fredericton, NB: Fiddlehead Poetry Books, 1979.

———. *Winter Songs*. London, ON: Killaly Press, 1977.

Wilson, Alan R. *Counting to 100*. Toronto, ON: Wolsak and Wynn, 1996.

———. *Animate Objects*. Winnipeg, MB: Turnstone Press, 1995.

ACKNOWLEDGEMENTS

The editors and publishers would like to thank the authors and publishers for their kind permission to use the poems in this anthology:

Milton Acorn, "I've Tasted My Blood," "Charlottetown Harbour," "The Island," "The Squall," and "That Corrugated Look to Water," *Dig Up My Heart* (McClelland & Stewart, 1983), and "The Completion of the Fiddle," *Captain Neal MacDougal & the Naked Goddess* (Ragweed, 1982), used with permission of the estate of Milton J.R. Acorn. Tammy Armstrong, "Presque Isle, Maine," "Wood Stove Sunday," "Boat Builder," and "Mother's Winter Guests," *Bogman's Music* (Anvil, 2001), used with permission of Anvil Press; "Horse Girls," used with per-mission of the author. Alfred G. Bailey, "The Unreturning," "The Isosceles Lighthouse," and "La Route Jackman," *Miramichi Lightning* (Fiddlehead Poetry Books, 1981), used with permission of the Bailey family; "Rivière du Loup," *The Sun, the Wind, the Summer Field* (Goose Lane, 1996), used with per-mission of Goose Lane Editions. Brian Bartlett, "Always" and "A Basement Tale," *Granite Erratics* (Ekstasis, 1997), used with permission of Ekstasis Editions; "to a northern gannet" and "The Afterlife of Trees," *The Afterlife of Trees* (McGill-Queen's UP, 2002), used with permission of McGill-Queen's University Press. Elizabeth Bishop, "At the Fishhouses," "Cape Breton," and "Poem," *The Complete Poems 1927-1979* (Farrar, Straus & Giroux, 1979), used with permission of Farrar, Straus & Giroux. Lesley-Anne Bourne, "Out of the Blizzard," *The Story of Pears* (Penumbra, 1990), and "The Boy I Never Met," "She Sends Him a Postcard of the Sea," and "Teaching My Husband to Swim," *Field Day* (Penumbra, 1996), used with permission of Penumbra Press. Elizabeth Brewster, "Where I Come From" and "Return of the Native," *Selected Poems of Elizabeth Brewster, Volume 1, 1944-77* (Oberon, 1985), and "The Moving Image," *footnotes to the book of job* (Oberon, 1995), used with permission of Oberon Press. Charles Bruce, "Nova Scotia Fish Hut," "Early Morning Landing," and "Orchard in the Woods," *The Mulgrave Road* (Macmillan, 1951), used by permission of the estate of Charles Bruce. George Elliott Clarke, "Haligonian Market Cry," *Execution Poems* (Gaspereau, 2001), used with permission of Gaspereau Press, Printers and Publishers; "Love Poem/Song Regarding Weymouth Falls," *Lush Dreams, Blue Exile: Fugitive Poems, 1978-1993* (Pottersfield, 1994), used with permission of the author; "Blank Sonnet," *Whylah Falls* (Polestar, 1990), and "Blue Elegies: I.v," *Blue* (Polestar, 2001), used with permission of Polestar, an Imprint of Raincoast Books. Fred Cogswell, "Valley-Folk," "George Burroughs," and "The Water and the Rock," *A Long Apprenticeship* (Fiddlehead Poetry Books, 1980), and "The Beach at Noon," *Meditations: 50 Sestinas* (Ragweed, 1986), used with permission of the author. Geoffrey Cook, "Chopping Wood," "Watermarks," and "Lorne, Nova Scotia," used with permission of the author. Allan Cooper, "After Rain," *To An Unborn Child* (Leaping Mountain, 1988), used with per-mission of the author; "The Worker Bee," *Singing the Flowers Open* (Gaspereau, 2001), used with permission of Gaspereau Press, Printers and Publishers. Michael Crummey, "What's Lost," "Capelin Scull," and "Painting the Islands,"

Hard Light (Brick, 1998), used with permission of Brick Books; "Loom," *Salvage* (McClelland & Stewart, 2002), used with permission of McClelland & Stewart Ltd. *The Canadian Publishers*. Mary Dalton, "Burn" and "The Marriage," used with permission of the author. Lynn Davies, "In the Beginning," "Cape Enrage," "When Ships Sail Too Close," "When You Can't Leave Me Anymore," and "On the Train," *The Bridge That Carries the Road* (Brick, 1999), used with permission of Brick Books. Tom Dawe, "Abandoned Outport," *Island Spell* (Harry Cuff, 1981), used with permission of the author and Harry Cuff Publications; "If Sonnets Were in Fashion," "Daedalus," and "Riddle," *In Hardy Country* (Breakwater, 1993), used with permission of Breakwater Books. Don Domanski, "Banns" and "Child of the Earth," *Parish of the Physic Moon* (McClelland & Stewart, 1998), used with permission of McClelland & Stewart, *The Canadian Publishers*; "Drowning Water," used by permission of the author. Robert Gibbs, "A Kind of Wakefulness" and "The Death of My Father," *The Tongue Still Dances* (Goose Lane, 1985), used with permission of Goose Lane Editions; "All This Night Long," *All This Night Long* (Fiddlehead Poetry Books, 1978), "The Manes P. Aground Off Fort Dufferin," *Earth Charms Heard So Early* (Fiddlehead Poetry Books, 1970), and "This Catching of Breath at the Top," *Earth Aches* (Wild East, 1991), used with permission of the author. Susan Goyette, "The True Names of Birds," "The moon on Friday night," and "The Peonies," *The True Names of Birds* (Brick, 1998), used with permission of Brick Books; "On Building a Nest," used with permission of the author. Richard Greene, "Crossing the Straits," and "Utopia," *Republic of Solitude* (Breakwater, 1994), used with permission of the author. Elisabeth Harvor, "Four O'Clock, New Year's Morning, New River Beach," *Fortress of Chairs* (Signal, 1992), and "The Damp Hips of the Women," *The Long Cold Green Evenings of Spring* (Signal, 1997), used with permission of Signal Editions/Véhicule Press. David Helwig, "Departures," "On the Island," and "Cape Breton in Autumn," *This Human Day* (Oberon, 2000), used with permission of Oberon Press. Rita Joe, "Passamaquoddy Song of the Stars," *Song of Eskasoni: More Poems of Rita Joe* (Ragweed, 1988); "You, I, Love, Beauty, Earth" and "Old Stories," *Lnu and Indians We're Called* (Ragweed, 1991), reprinted by permission of Canadian Scholars' Press, Inc., Women's Press and/or gynergy books; "Plawej and L'nui'site'w," *We Are the Dreamers* (Breton Books, 1999), used with permission of Breton Books. M. Travis Lane, "Codicil" and "For Brigid," *Keeping Afloat* (Guernica, 2001), used with permission of Guernica Editions; "Poem Upon the Forcible Entry by Cat into a Poem Originally Upon Trilliums," *Poems 1968-1972* (Fiddlehead Poetry Books, 1973); and "Portobello," used by permission of the author. Carole Glasser Langille, "Prayer," "Scanning an Afternoon in Winter," "Through a Slit in the Tent," and "The Sadness of Windows," *In Cannon Cave* (Brick, 1997), used with permission of Brick Books. Richard Lemm, "Metamorphosis," "Spark," and "Perfect Circle," *four ways of dealing with bullies* (Wolsak and Wynn, 2000), used with permission of the author and Wolsak and Wynn Publishers; "My Class Draws a Blank on Robbie Burns," *Prelude to the Bacchanal* (Ragweed, 1990), used with permission of the author. Douglas Lochhead, "Nothing," *All Things Do Continue* (St. Thomas Poetry Series, 1997) and "The Cemetery at Loch End, Catalone, Cape Breton," *The Full Furnace: Collected Poems* (McGraw-Hill Ryerson, 1975), used with permission of the author;

"John Thompson," *Upper Cape Poems* (Goose Lane, 1989), used with permission of Goose Lane Editions. Jeanette Lynes, "The Fern Kidnappings," "The Valley, After Blossoms," "Muskoxen," "Brave," and "What We Learned on the Highway Near St. John's," used with permission of the author. Hugh MacDonald, "The Digging of Deep Wells" and "Shingle Flies," *The Digging of Deep Wells* (Black Moss, 1997), used with permission of Black Moss Press. John MacKenzie, "Me as an Archaeologist," "Sledgehammer," "My love is strung with the ancient," and "Hearthouse," *Sledgehammer* (Polestar, 2000) used with permission of Polestar, an Imprint of Raincoast Books. Brent MacLaine, "Making the Middle Be," *Wind and Root* (Signal, 2000), used with permission of Signal Editions/ Véhicule Press; "North Shore Park" and "Birth Story," *Where the Branch Bends*, used by permission of the author. Sue MacLeod, "when night meets thread & needle & lies down among the bedclothes," "especially after rain, the gulls," and "This is the body, consoling itself," used by permission of the author. Randall Maggs, "Tropical Toads," *Timely Departures* (Breakwater, 1994), "Night Crossing in Ice," and "Signal Hill," used by permission of the author. Carmelita McGrath, "Let Us Go and Find a Place to Worship," *To the New World* (Killick, 1997), "Solar Eclipse, St. John's, Newfoundland," "Booman," and "How to Leave an Island," used by permission of the author. Robert Moore, "From *The Golden Book of Bovinities*," "Room with a view," and "The Skin You Wore," *So Rarely in Our Skins* (Muses' Company, 2002), used with permission of The Muses' Company/J. Gordon Shillingford Publishing. Alden Nowlan, "The Red Wool Shirt," *Smoked Glass* (Clarke Irwin, 1977), and "Day's End," "And He Wept Aloud, . . ." "Britain Street," and "Daughter of Zion," *Bread, Wine and Salt* (Clarke Irwin, 1967), used with permission of Stoddart Publishing; Thomas O'Grady, "Dark Horses," "Cormorants," "Some Day, Paradise," and "A Prayer for My Daughters," *What Really Matters* (McGill-Queen's UP, 2000), used with permission of McGill-Queen's University Press. Al Pittman, "Another Night in Crawley's Cove," *Dancing the Limbo* (Breakwater, 1993), and "Lupines," *Thirty for Sixty* (Breakwater, 1999), used with permission of Breakwater Books. matt robinson, "a move to liquid" and "snow; a fear of dying," *a ruckus of awkward stacking* (Insomniac, 2001), used with permission of Insomniac Press; "a winter's affection; radiomimetic" and "the body as dictionary, as bible," *how we play at it: a list* (ECW, forthcoming), used with permission of ECW Press. Gordon Rodgers, "The Laboratory," *The Pyrate Latitudes* (Creative, 1986); and "White Wedding," "Drowned," and "On the Ice," *Floating Houses* (Creative, 1984), used with permission of the author. Peter Sanger, "Heron," *The America Reel* (Pottersfield, 1983), used by permission of the author; "Escalade," "Kestrel," "Crabapple Blossoms," and "Woodcock Feather," *Earth Moth* (Goose Lane, 1991), used with permission of Goose Lane Editions. Joseph Sherman, "For Mordecai Richler's Shalinksy Who Said 'A Jew Is an Idea,'" *Chaim the Slaughterer* (Oberon, 1974), and "Aphelion" and "My Father Plaits His Granddaughter's Hair," *American Standard* (Oberon, 2001), used by permission of Oberon Press. Anne Simpson, "Deer on a Beach" and "White, Mauve, Yellow," *Light Falls Through You* (McClelland & Stewart, 2000), and "A Name, Many Names" and "The Lilacs," *Timepiece* (McClelland & Stewart, 2002), used with permission of McClelland & Stewart Ltd. *The Canadian Publishers*. Sue Sinclair, "Red Pepper" and "Saturday Afternoon," *Secrets of Weather & Hope* (Brick, 2001), used with permission of Brick Books; "Orpheus Meets Eurydice in the Underworld," "Lilacs," "The Refrigerator," and "Paddling," used with permission of the author. Douglas Burnet Smith, "Bare Places," "Walk After Rain," and "Skull," *Ladder to the Moon* (Brick, 1988), used with permission of Brick Books; "Multiple Choice," *Voices From a Farther Room* (Wolsak and Wynn, 1992), and "untitled" from *The Killed* (Wolsak and Wynn, 2000), used with permission of Wolsak and Wynn Publishers. John Smith, "The unicorn," *Fireflies in the Magnolia*; "The muted," *Midnight Found You Dancing* (Ragweed, 1986); and "You Wanted to Hear," "Early Morning Was," "All Light," and "How Could They," *Strands the Length of the Wind* (Ragweed, 1993), used with permission of the author. Kay Smith, "On Sundays in Summer" and "Again with Music," *When a Girl Looks Down* (Fiddlehead Poetry Books, 1978); "Remembering Miller" and "Old Women and Love," *The Bright Particulars* (Ragweed, 1987), used with permission of the author. Andrew Steeves, "Winter Marsh" and "Haunting," *Cutting the Devil's Throat* (Goose Lane, 1998), used with permission of Goose Lane Editions. John Steffler, "They all gave one last squirt," *The Grey Islands* (Brick, 2000), used with permission of Brick Books; "Cedar Cove" and "That Night We Were Ravenous," *That Night We Were Ravenous* (McClelland & Stewart, 1998), used with permission of McClelland & Stewart Ltd. *The Canadian Publishers*. Fraser Sutherland, "Undergoing," "On the Beach One Day," and "Auden's Face," *Madwomen* (Black Moss, 1978), used with permission of Black Moss Press. John Thompson, "Horse," "Turnip Field," and "The Onion," *At the Edge of the Chopping There Are No Secrets* (Anansi, 1973), and "Ghazal I," and "Ghazal XXXVII," *Stilt Jack* (Anansi, 1978), used with permission of Stoddart Publishing. Michael Thorpe, "Open-Air Museum" and "Wishful Fall," *Out of the Storm* (Penumbra, 1984), used with permission of Penumbra Press; "Presence and Process," *Bagdad Is Everywhere* (TSAR, 1991), used with permission of TSAR Publications. Harry Thurston, "Father on My Shoulders" and "Revelations," *Clouds Flying Before the Eye* (Fiddlehead Poetry Books & Goose Lane, 1985), used with permission of the author; "River Otters at Play" and "Dragging Bottom," *If Men Lived on Earth* (Gaspereau, 2000), used with permission of Gaspereau Press, Printers and Publishers. Eric Trethewey, "The Text of Evening," "Homesteading," "Green Cadillac," and "Resurrection at West Lake," *The Long Road Home* (Goose Lane, 1994), used with permission of Goose Lane Editions. R.M. Vaughan, "10 Reasons Why I Fall in Love with Inaccessible Straight Boys Every Damn Time" and "insight into private affairs . . . ," *A Selection of Dazzling Scarves* (ECW, 1996), and "Men Together" and "Simone Signoret, Beldam," *Invisible to Predators* (ECW, 1999), used with permission of ECW Press. Agnes Walsh, "The Time That Passes" and "Night in the Ashes," *In the Old Country of My Heart* (Killick, 1996); and "The Tilts, Point Lance" and "Mike's," used with permission of the author. Patrick Warner, "Poem without Beginning or End," "The Crocus (after snow)," and "The Heart," *All Manner of Misunderstanding* (Killick, 2001), used with permission of Killick Press. Enos Watts, "Summer Solstice," "Longliner at Sunset," and "Crocuses and Crown-of-Thorns," *Autumn Vengeance* (Breakwater, 1986), used with permission of Breakwater Books. Liliane Welch, "In Cézanne's Studio," *Unlearning Ice* (Borealis, 2001), "Claude Monet's Water Landscapes" and "Dikes on Funday

Bay," *The Rock's Stillness* (Borealis, 1999), and "Tattoo," *Fidelities* (Borealis, 1997), used with permission of Borealis Press; "December 1972: First Winter Ascension of Sass Maor," *Manstorna* (Ragweed, 1985), used with permission of the author. Alan R. Wilson, "Antlia the Air Pump," "Pegasus the Winged Horse," "Lynx," and "Octans the Octant," used with permission of the author.

The editors wish to thank many people for their enthusiastic support. For two years, matt robinson, a graduate assistant at the University of New Brunswick, worked on this anthology, developing bibliographic and biographical materials for us. We are most grateful for his help. Charmaine Cadeau and David Hickey, Creative Writing MA students at UNB, assisted with proofreading. Mary Dalton was a valuable advisor, making suggestions for selections and creating and checking bibliographies. Poets and teachers in the Atlantic area, among them Brian Bartlett, Mary Brodkorb, George Elliott Clarke, Stan Dragland, Richard Lemm, Brent MacLaine, and John Steffler, offered valuable suggestions.

Above all, we wish to acknowledge the advice, support, and editorial acumen of Laurel Boone, who encouraged us all the way through. Thanks to all those at Goose Lane Editions who contributed to the project.

INDEX

BP